The Everyday Gourmet
Rediscovering the Lost
Art of Cooking

Bill Briwa, C.E.C., C.H.E.

PUBLISHED BY:

THE GREAT COURSES
Corporate Headquarters
4840 Westfields Boulevard, Suite 500
Chantilly, Virginia 20151-2299
Phone: 1-800-832-2412
Fax: 703-378-3819
www.thegreatcourses.com

Bill Briwa, C.E.C., C.H.E.
Chef-Instructor
The Culinary Institute of America
at Greystone

A 1980 graduate of The Culinary Institute of America (CIA), Chef Bill Briwa has worked in the hospitality industry for over 30 years and is a Certified Executive Chef and Certified Hospitality Educator. In addition to being the resident chef for The Hess Collection winery in California's Napa Valley, Chef Briwa owned and operated his own bistro and worked at Thomas Keller's award-winning restaurant The French Laundry. He was also the executive chef for The Wine Spectator Restaurant at The CIA at Greystone and served as an officer on the board of the St. Helena Farmers' Market. As culinary chair of the 2004 Napa Valley Wine Auction, Chef Briwa helped raise more than five million dollars for local charities. In addition to his work as a cook and chef, he has worked as both a baker and pastry chef. His writing on food and wine, olive oil, and cooking has been featured locally and in *Fine Cooking, Mise en Place*, and *Sunset* as well as in the trade publications *Flavor & the Menu* and *Practical Winery & Vineyard Journal*.

As a Chef-Instructor at the CIA, Chef Briwa has developed curricula and has taught cooking, flavor dynamics, gastronomy, and food-and-wine pairing full time for the past 15 years. He has traveled to both teach and study cooking across the United States and to China, Mexico, South and Central America, Europe, and around the Mediterranean. In addition, he is part of the Industry Services Group at the CIA and works closely with a broad range of corporate clients to help them realize their culinary goals.

Chef Briwa has been a speaker at many professional conferences, and he takes part in the Healthy Kitchens, Healthy Lives conference held twice each year at The CIA at Greystone. The conference is copresented by Harvard School of Public Health and the CIA. Chef Briwa has collaborated with

Dr. Connie Guttersen, an instructor at the CIA and author of *The Sonoma Diet*, on numerous presentations on nutrition and cooking, including a course on the science of healthy cooking produced by The Great Courses. In 2003, Chef Briwa was a judge for the American Cheese Society, and in 2005, he presented on gastronomy at the annual conference of the International Association of Culinary Professionals (IACP). In 2005, 2006, and 2007, he presented at the International Foodservice Manufacturers Association's (IFMA) Chain Operators Exchange (COEX) conference, and in 2008 and 2009, he spoke at the National Restaurant Association (NRA) Show in Chicago, Illinois. Chef Briwa also presented at Beyond Extra Virgin IV, a conference on superpremium olive oil, in Verona, Italy.

Over the last 30 years of cooking and teaching, Chef Briwa has taken one short break from the stove to become a puppeteer. He lives in Yountville, California, with his wife and a border collie—both of whom think highly of his cooking. ∎

Table of Contents

iv

Table of Contents

SUPPLEMENTAL MATERIAL

This course focuses on cooking techniques, ingredients, and flavor. Shopping lists for ingredients are included, but the proportions will be up to you! Our Chef-Instructor encourages you to taste and experiment to become a more confident and competent cook.

Cooking—Ingredients, Technique, and Flavor
Lesson 1

O ver the course of the following 24 lessons, you will learn foundational cooking techniques that will open up a broader world of food and cooking for your enjoyment. The goal of this comprehensive program is to help you become a better cook—one that is more confident, more aware, and more likely to draw satisfaction from the craft of preparing food. This program is based on three broad themes. The first is understanding that ingredients have to be of good quality and that you can only expect those ingredients to do certain things. The second broad theme is learning some foundational cooking techniques. Finally, it is important that you understand the interaction of taste and flavor, which is the focus of this lesson.

The Interaction of Taste and Flavor

All human beings have an opening—our mouth—through which every bit of the food that we eat passes. Our mouth is artificially moistened with saliva, and the moisture of saliva facilitates swallowing. Saliva also has antimicrobial properties that protect us. Furthermore, we can't taste unless the things that we are eating begin to dissolve, and the enzymes in saliva break down food.

Our mouth has taste buds on our tongue and palate, and those taste buds have the ability to perceive the five basic tastes: sweet, sour, salty, bitter, and savory. The five basic tastes are meaningful. They are markers for things that have assured our survival since the beginning of mankind.

Sweetness is a marker for ripeness in fruits and vegetables. When we taste sweetness, which we are predisposed to like, we respond positively. When sweetness is available to us, such as when we encounter a bush of ripe raspberries, we are encouraged to fill our bodies with carbohydrates, which provide energy for our existence.

Saltiness is a marker for sodium, which we need to regulate our bodily functions, but it is also a marker for micronutrients and minerals.

Sourness is a marker for underripeness—or even spoilage. Sourness is a warning signal that alerts us to stop eating a certain food. This mechanism is what keeps us from eating too many green apples and getting a stomachache.

1

Bitterness is a marker for alkaloids. In a plant-based diet, alkaloids are often poisonous. Bitterness warns us that we are eating a food that might be risky to eat.

Savory flavors are the most difficult to describe and to understand. Savoriness, or what the Japanese call umami, is the flavor of protein that has begun to break down a little bit through enzyme activity or through long cooking. Savory flavors can be found in soy sauce, cured meats, blue cheese, and aged cheeses.

There is an important distinction between taste and flavor. Taste is the five things that you taste on your tongue, and flavor is those five things plus your ability to perceive aroma. In other words, taste plus aroma equals flavor. For example, a ripe melon has a wonderful, floral scent, but that floral scent is more than just sweet. In addition, a well-made cappuccino has a roasted flavor that is so much more than just a dark, bitter liquid.

One of the great things about recognizing the distinction between taste and flavor is that when you are in the kitchen seasoning food, most of your challenges have to do with the interaction of tastes with one another. Cooking is not really about esoteric herbs and spices; it simply boils down to sweet, sour, salty, bitter, and savory.

Taste + Aroma = Flavor

Try eating a jelly bean while plugging your nose, which takes away your ability to smell. It doesn't matter what flavor the jelly bean is; in fact, it is better if you don't know what the flavor is. Plug your nose, and eat it, and along the way, try to decide what you notice about the flavor of the jelly bean. You should notice that it is sweet and that it has a characteristic texture. In addition, you might detect a little acidity, but quite frankly, you shouldn't be able to tell what flavor it is.

As soon as you unplug your nose, the flavor of the jelly bean should immediately become apparent. In addition, when you unplug your nose, the distinction between taste and flavor should become apparent. In other words, taste and aroma equal the flavor that you perceive.

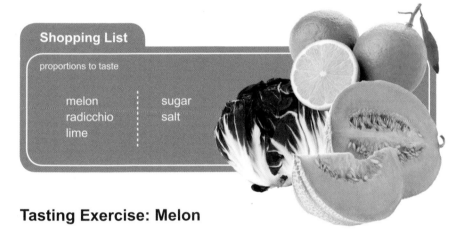

Shopping List

proportions to taste

melon	sugar
radicchio	salt
lime	

Tasting Exercise: Melon

As you participate in the following tasting exercises, take small bites. You don't need to eat a lot of any of the food, and there will be several opportunities for you to taste them in various combinations.

Gather everything that you need for this exercise so that you are prepared. The French would call this *mise en place*, or everything in place. You can also think of it as having your mess in place.

Start by taking a small bite of melon. Obviously, melon is sweet. If you smell a floral aroma, or muskiness, that is an indicator that the melon is ripe—as is the level of sugar, the texture, and the juiciness. If the melon is heavy, then it is moist with juice.

Sweetness is a marker for ripeness, but it is very subtle. Dip the melon into sugar, and then taste it again. The excess sugar may fool you for a second, but when you start to recognize that the texture and aroma aren't equal to that level of sugar, then you recognize that something is amiss.

About a third of people love to salt melon. If you put a little bit of salt on your melon—just enough to give it a little seasoning—it might surprise you that you have a much fuller taste experience. It is more satisfying, and it might even surprise you that the melon actually tastes a little sweeter. It lingers longer on your palate. For some reason, it seems more enjoyable.

Your Mouth Is a Laboratory

Anthelme Brillat-Savarin, a famous French food writer who lived in the 1800s, said that the human mouth is like a laboratory, and that laboratory has the ability to perceive the basic tastes. Coming off of that laboratory is a chimney—your nose—which has the ability to perceive all things aromatic. Those two things in tandem with one another give you the ability to perceive and enjoy flavor.

Imagine that you are traveling to Mexico on vacation, and in the morning, there is melon laid out for breakfast. Aside the melon is some lime juice. If you season the melon with a few drops of lime juice, you will have a fuller experience. The sweetness of the melon is tempered by the acidity of the lime juice. In addition, there is a tremendous aroma to the lime that is the result of the fruit having ripened, and that aroma mingles with the muskiness of the melon, and it seems somehow riper by having a fuller aroma.

Tasting Exercise: Radicchio

Next, taste some radicchio by itself. The bitter flavor is almost like a warning device that tells you that you are eating something that is risky and that if you swallow it, it may do you some harm because there is a chance that it is poisonous. It's surprising that you taste bitterness most acutely at the very back of your palate—almost as if mother nature is trying to give you one last chance to notice that the food is bitter and that if you swallow it, it's your fault that you poisoned yourself.

When you taste the radicchio, you will find that it's not particularly pleasant. A good strategy for dealing with bitterness in food is to add sugar to it. For example, some people like bitter coffee with sugar in it.

Put a little bit of sugar on the radicchio, and notice an initial sweetness, but as that sweetness passes off of your palate, the bitterness actually seems more intense by comparison to the sweetness. When you have a type of food that has an inherent sweetness, then sweetness is maybe a good strategy for enhancing the flavor, but there's no sweetness in radicchio.

Instead of sugar, put a little bit of salt on the radicchio, and suddenly, there is a resonance. The bitterness is still there, but there's something about seasoning it with salt that makes the flavor fuller and less aggressive.

Next, put a few drops of lime on the radicchio, tasting it with just acidity. Think of the lime juice as a salad dressing. When you add it to the bitter green, it actually tastes pretty good. The acidity is assertive enough to stand up to the bitterness and push it down a little bit. When you eat radicchio on its own, it's the star, but side by side with acidity, it becomes one of the supporting layers in the flavor experience.

Tying It All Together

Imagine that you are going to open a restaurant, and on that restaurant's menu will be a salad that has bitter greens and melon with a dressing made of lime juice. Take a small little bite of melon and a piece of radicchio and dress the combination with four or five drops of lime juice. Season it with salt; the flavors are big, so the salt has to be assertive. Then, punch up some of the sweetness of the melon with sugar. If you like your food spicy, try adding a few grains of cayenne pepper. Don't overdo it because you don't want to blow your palate away.

Gather all of the elements of your salad, and in one mouthful, close your eyes, chew it, and evaluate the flavor experience. You will notice that the experience is very full. You taste the bitter greens and the sweetness of the melon. You smell the aroma of the melon and the lime. You taste sweetness, saltiness, and a little bit of heat, or irritation, coming from the cayenne (if you added it).

With this salad, you have jangled all of your taste receptors—those for sweet, sour, salty, and bitter—which have all been brought to life. Beyond this being a full tasting experience, if you had to re-create it, you could interchange these food items almost infinitely and come up with a flavor experience that soothes your taste.

The idea of tasting, evaluating, and then adjusting is incredibly important. It is a skill that you will use in the kitchen again and again. As you tasted the salad, you might have wished that you had added just a few more drops of lime, and to accompany that lime, a few more grains of salt to really punch up the flavor in a nice way. Perhaps the amount of sugar and cayenne that you used was just right. The subtleties of the interaction of taste and flavor are incredibly important when cooking.

Don't waste any time wishing that you were a better taster. Instead, put your effort into becoming a better taster through focused attention and curiosity every time you prepare, season, and eat food. This skill set is foundational. It will serve you well every day of your life, and the payoff is more enjoyment and pleasure every time you sit down to eat.

Your Most Essential Tool—Knives

Lesson 2

Contrary to what you might think, your cutting board and knives can be your friends. Cutting vegetables does not have to be tedious and messy. In fact, if you focus on the job at hand and tune everything else out, then cutting vegetables can even be therapeutic. Every recipe that you use will call for vegetables to be prepared slightly differently, so it is important to be familiar with the various types of knives and what they are used for. Knives are quite possibly the most important piece of equipment that you will use in the kitchen.

Types of Kitchen Knives

Knives are like fountain pens; you want one that feels good in your hand. Don't spend a lot of money on knives until you have had the chance to work with some and figure out which types you like.

A forged knife is made by taking a hot piece of steel and forging the shape of the blade and handle. Then, wood is attached. A stamped knife starts as a sheet of steel that is stamped into the shape of the blade. Then, the handle is affixed and an edge is put on it. Stamped knives cost much less than what a forged knife costs. In addition, a forged knife is a little bit heavier, and the steel is harder.

Many older knives are made from carbon steel, and the downside to carbon steel is that it is reactive, so it will rust and discolor unless you are very careful to wipe it clean and make sure there are no corrosives on it.

Today, most knives are made from high-carbon stainless steel. If you invest in a good high-carbon knife, make sure you are committed to wiping the moisture and any corrosives off the blade every time you use it. Otherwise, the knife will tarnish or rust.

Choosing a Cutting Board

A cutting board is an essential piece of equipment that you will use in the kitchen every day. A large wooden cutting board is best because it is solid, so it won't move around when you are cutting, and because the surface area is large enough so that you don't feel crowded. If you use a smaller cutting board that is made from a manmade material, as your knife passes over the board, it will feel like the board is dulling the knife.

Basic Knives

In the kitchen, you need the right tool for the job. The chef's knife, or the French knife, is used for all the tasks that take place on the cutting board. The knife has a wonderful curve in it that makes it smooth when you work with it. If that curve has been ground out of it, then the knife won't work smoothly.

A paring knife is another good knife to have on hand. Paring knives can be relatively inexpensive, but you can also buy a paring knife that is made by forging the blade, and the price of that knife can often be 40 or 50 dollars. Too often, paring knives get swept up and end up in the garbage, so don't spend a tremendous amount of money on them. More important than the quality of the blade—or even whether it is forged or stamped—is the fact that the blade is sharp.

A utility knife typically has a shorter blade than a chef's knife. Some people call utility knives tomato knives or sandwich knives.

A boning knife is great for butchery, taking apart a chicken, or cleaning a beef fillet. It is often on the thinner side, and it is handy if the blade is flexible. A flexible blade allows you to push the knife against something solid, such as a bone, without losing any meat in the process.

A fillet knife is used for filleting fish, and it also has a flexible blade so that you can press it against a bone without leaving any meat behind. A fillet knife is handy if you do a lot of fishing.

A slicing knife has a very long, thin blade that tends to be very sharp. Because it has such a thin blade, it doesn't stick to food very well. When you are carving a roast beef, for example, you might want to use a slicing knife with a sharp edge.

A serrated knife has little teeth on it that allow for the cutting of tomatoes, for example, which sometimes resist the edge of your knife if it is not sharp. It's very difficult for a knife with a smooth blade to cut through the crusty loaf of bread, so you would use a serrated knife in that case as well.

A vegetable peeler is a very handy thing to have in the kitchen; it is nothing more than a knife and a steel.

A cleaver is a nonessential knife for the home kitchen that you would only need if you have to cut through bones. However, while it can cut through bones, it can also destroy your chopping blocks.

Dicing Onions

To dice an onion, if you are using a cutting board, use a chef's knife, but if you are not using a cutting board, use a paring knife. Start by cutting off the root end and then the stem end so that you can peel it. However, be careful not to

cut all of the root end off. Onions are made up of circles that all come together at the root end, so the onion will fall apart if you cut all of it off.

One of the big challenges with onions is that it's a round vegetable that likes to roll around. To give it a flat side that it can rest on, cut between the root end and the stem end by sliding the knife through the onion—don't just press down.

Being Safe with Knives

When using knives in your kitchen, remember that knives are sharp tools, and they can be dangerous. When you rest a knife on your cutting board, make sure that it is in plain sight; be careful not to cover it accidentally and then forget where it is hiding because you could hurt yourself when you find it. In addition, don't let the edge of the blade hang off the edge of your cutting board because someone walking by might run into it. If you have to move through the kitchen with a knife, hold it down by your side rather than gesturing with it. If a knife on your cutting board gets knocked off, don't reach out and try to catch it; instead, just step back and let it clatter to the floor. Breaking the tip off of a knife is far preferable to cutting the tip off of a finger.

Put the root end down on the cutting board. If you want to dice an onion into chunks that are a quarter of an inch on a side, make cuts on the top of the onion that are a quarter of an inch thick that go almost all the way through—but not all the way through—the bottom of the onion. You want to leave the root end untouched so that everything remains held together. Then, turn the onion 90 degrees and make one cut horizontally to the board almost all the way through. Finally, make quarter-inch cuts at a 90-degree angle to the cuts you made originally.

When you are done making quarter-inch cuts, you can finally cut the root end off so that the onion falls apart. Cut it radially, with the knife pointing toward the center, and the onion will fall apart into what is, in effect, a little julienne.

Julienning Potatoes

If you ever want to practice cutting, use a potato because it is inexpensive and it also involves putting a flat side on it—just as you did with the onion.

If you want to make a julienne, which involves cuts that are about a 16th of an inch on a side, start by cutting a slice that is just a 16th of an inch thick, and then stack up the slices. Keep your fingertips tucked away, allowing the side of the blade to ride on your knuckle, and as you pull your knuckle back, the blade should follow it in the form of a nice, smooth rocking motion.

If you started with a slice that was an eighth of an inch thick and then cut it in half and stacked the slices, you would have something that the French call an *allumette*, or a matchstick-sized cut. In addition, if you started with a cut that was about a quarter of an inch thick—and about two to two and a half inches long—and then stacked the slices, you would have what the French call a *batonnet*, or a cut that looks like a baton.

Cutting Carrots

The blade on a vegetable peeler is designed to take off a very thin strip of carrot. One of the challenges with a carrot is that because it's thick on one end and very thin on the other, it is difficult for it to cook evenly. The oblique cut, or the roll cut, makes the pieces more uniform in size. Cut the top and bottom off of the carrot and discard them. Then, make a diagonal cut, roll the carrot, make another diagonal cut, and carry on that way. As you get closer to the top, you don't have to cut so deeply.

If you want a very fine dice, put a flat side on the carrot and then cut about an eighth of an inch thick (the start of *allumette*) and stack the slices. Cut them into very small eighth-inch dice. This is a cut called *brunoise*, and it's a decorative cut. You would not use this cut for making a chicken stock, but you would use it for a dish in which you want the vegetables to show.

Slicing and Smashing Garlic

The easiest technique for peeling a few cloves of garlic involves cutting the tough stem end off of the garlic and then using the knife to crush the garlic very lightly, which should loosen the skin enough so that it will peel right off.

Once the garlic is peeled, you have some options. You can slice the garlic, which would be appropriate in a rustic preparation. The finer the work, the more you work toward the tip of the blade; the coarser the work, the more you work toward the heel of the blade. Slicing the garlic would result in large chunks of garlic, and when you cook it, it would give off a lot of flavor.

You could also smash the garlic with the side of the blade and then gather it up and chop it, taking advantage of the curve in the blade and rocking the knife over the top of the garlic. Use the blade to gather the pieces as they spread across the chopping board. Chop it as fine or as coarsely as you like. Be careful to keep all of your fingers on top of the blade.

Sharpening Your Knives

With a nice selection of knives, it doesn't matter whether they are forged or stamped—what really matters is that they are sharp. Therefore, it is best to have your knives professionally sharpened. Once they have been sharpened, you need to commit to keeping them sharp. A knife block offers a nice way to protect the edges of your knives, or if you want to keep your knives loose in a kitchen drawer, use a little plastic sleeve that can protect the edge of a knife when it is not in use.

Chopping Parsley

When chopping parsley, first get most of the stems out of the way; you can save those for adding to stocks or soups. Parsley can seem a little ungainly on the cutting board; it takes up a lot of room and is hard to keep under control. Gather it up, and be a little aggressive with it. Bring it together into a little ball, and hold it with your fingertips. Keeping your fingertips tucked underneath, cut through the ball of parsley once with your knife to get the unruly mass of parsley under control.

For a rustic preparation, one cut through the parsley is enough. For a finer preparation, you might want to cut it until it's very difficult to see the individual pieces of parsley. However, the more you cut, the more damaged the parsley becomes, and it will start to get a little bit watery. If it's so watery that you can no longer sprinkle it, you can wrap it in the end of a kitchen towel and wring the juice out of it.

As you do this work, it's good to have a towel on hand because sooner or later, you're going to discover that you want to be able to wipe your knife off or wipe your cutting board clean.

The Chiffonade Technique

For a leafy vegetable or herb like basil, a technique called chiffonade involves stacking the leaves into a little pile and then rolling the pile up as if it were a cigar. Then, you cut the cigar into little threads, or ribbons. When you chop both basil and mint, they quickly turn black because there are enzymes in them that don't react well when exposed to oxygen. This technique is the least invasive way of dealing with these herbs, and it guarantees that the herb will hold for a long time and not turn black.

Baked Minestrone Soup

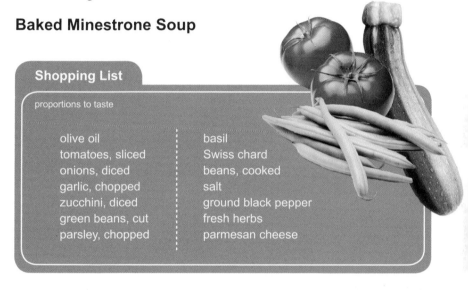

Shopping List

proportions to taste

olive oil	basil
tomatoes, sliced	Swiss chard
onions, diced	beans, cooked
garlic, chopped	salt
zucchini, diced	ground black pepper
green beans, cut	fresh herbs
parsley, chopped	parmesan cheese

The best way to get rid of a bunch of vegetables that are sitting in your refrigerator is to make a soup. Whenever you are cutting vegetables to put into a soup, keep in mind that somebody is going to have to eat the soup off of a spoon, and if the cut is too large to fit on a spoon, then it will be difficult to eat.

Start by heating a pan on the stove and adding some olive oil to the bottom. Then, slice some tomatoes and add them to the pan. As the soup cooks, the tomatoes will start to fall apart, lending their flavor and moisture to the soup. Once there is a layer of tomatoes on the bottom, add some diced onions and chopped garlic.

Next, add some diced zucchini. Cut each zucchini lengthwise and then into quarters; then, dice it. In addition, cut some green beans into inch-long pieces.

Then, add some chopped parsley and some basil chiffonade. You can use the technique of chiffonade on a large scale with some Swiss chard that you slice into big ribbons. Add those to the pan.

Later, you will add some beans to the soup, but the beans will have cooked already, so you don't need to add them at the beginning because they are already tender. However, the liquid that the beans cooked in can be added to the pan of vegetables. Stir the liquid before adding it, however, because there's a lot of starch in there that will give body to the soup. Pour the liquid just up to the bottom of the chard in the pan and season it with salt and pepper—plus a little more olive oil. Put a lid on the pan, turn up the heat, and bring it to a boil.

Once the soup boils, put it in the oven and cook it at about 400 or 450 degrees for about 20 minutes. Then, take it out of the oven and add the beans that have been drained of their liquid. Put it back into the oven for another 20 minutes. Once it comes out of the oven, it should sit for about 10 or 15 minutes just so that the flavors can mingle. Finish it with some fresh herbs and parmesan cheese. Finally, add a good-quality olive oil, something with a peppery bite.

Remember to taste the soup before serving it so that you can adjust its flavor if needed. You can also add other vegetables—including spinach to brighten it up—if you want. After making this soup, you can store it for a few days in the refrigerator, and it will keep well.

More Essential Tools— From Pots to Shears

Lesson 3

Unless you are really careful, you can quickly become overwhelmed with too many esoteric tools, pots, and pans in the kitchen. The trick is that you don't need a lot of tools—you just need the right tools. This lesson will help you select the tools that you need so that your kitchen becomes a friendlier, safer, more enjoyable place. The goal of this lesson is to move you toward a kitchen that works for you and for the food that you would like to cook in that kitchen.

Guidelines for Buying Kitchen Equipment

If you buy a new piece of equipment for your kitchen, notice how often you use it. A piece of equipment that gets used many times on a daily basis, such as a cutting board or knife, is an essential piece of equipment, and you should feel fine about spending a lot of money on those items to get exactly what you want. However, if you have a piece of equipment that you use once every few weeks, it might be a helpful item, but it's not essential. A piece of equipment that you only use every few months is perhaps an unnecessary piece of equipment for you to keep on hand in your kitchen. If you only use an item twice a year, it can live in the basement or garage so that it doesn't clutter up your life on a daily basis.

Pots and Pans

It's a good idea to have a selection of saucepans with tight-fitting lids. The larger ones should have two handles because they can get pretty unwieldy if they're full of food.

Nonstick pans are invaluable if you're cooking eggs. If you take good care of them and don't use them for anything else, the nonstick coating will last a long time.

A sauteuse—also known as a sauté pan or frying pan—has sloping sides, which are important because they allow you to flip food and move it very quickly over high heat.

A sautoir is a type of frying pan that has straight sides, is a little bit deeper, and has a tight-fitting lid. A sautoir is great if you want to fry a piece of chicken and then make a sauce right in the pan because you can put a lid on the pan and trap the steam.

Stockpots are pots that you might use for boiling pasta or cooking a lot of soup. A traditional stockpot in a professional kitchen is a narrower pot that is also deeper. A narrower, deeper pot takes up less room on the stove, and you don't get as much evaporation over a long period of cooking. When you're making soup, you might want a shallower pot that makes it easier to manipulate the food inside. With a shallower pot, you don't get as much steaming, which can prevent things from browning.

Stockpots often come with a few inserts. There is a perforated insert that sits on the top of the pot—with the water down below and a lid up above—and becomes a serviceable steamer. There is another insert that is perforated but is a little bit deeper. When you place it in the pot with boiling water, you could then add pasta to the pot, and then when it's time to take the pasta out of the water, simply lift the insert, allowing the water to drain from the pasta, and then add the pasta directly to the sauce. There are also pasta baskets that serve a similar purpose.

Many people use a colander for the purpose of draining the water from cooked pasta. When your pasta is ready, you put the colander in the sink and dump the

pasta into the colander. However, the downside to using a colander is that you lose the pasta water, which is a precious commodity that can be used to adjust consistencies and make really simple sauces. However, a colander is not a bad thing to have on hand in your kitchen.

You should have a selection of stainless-steel bowls, including a large one that might hold salad for about eight people and a small one that might be just right for making the salad dressing that goes on that salad. Salad bowls that are rounded on the bottom are great if you want to whip and manipulate the food in the bowl. On the other hand, if you're just mixing something up, then a flat-bottomed pan is fine. Then, there are bowls that are hybrids of the two that have flat bottoms, but the curved sides go almost all the way down to the center.

You should also have a selection of roasting pans, including a smaller one that would be appropriate if you were making a lasagna or roasting a chicken and a larger one that would be useful if you were roasting a turkey or prime rib.

There are a few nonessential but handy pans that you might want to consider having in your kitchen. A cast-iron pan that is seasoned and nonstick holds the heat very well. A braising pot that is oval is also helpful to have when making a pot roast because there's not a lot of extra room around the outside of the roast, and when it goes into the oven, the cast iron is so heavy that the heat is diffused and comes to the meat in a very even way.

Hand Tools and Smallwares

A balloon whip is great for whipping air into preparations like cream or egg whites. A sauce whip is composed of much heavier wires and a much narrower head. Because it has a narrower head, it more easily fits into the corners of a saucepan. A sauce whip would be appropriate for stirring flour and water into a sauce to make it thick.

A bain-marie insert contains a bath of hot water that is then inserted into a larger pot. It is used, for example, to keep soup warm.

It is helpful to have two sets of tongs—one that is short and one that is long. A short one is appropriate when you're doing fine work, but if you're cooking on a grill and the fire is hot, a longer set of tongs is useful so that you don't burn your hands.

Ladles are great for portioning soup or taking clarified butter and putting it into a hollandaise as it's being made. In addition, the size or volume of the ladle is typically written on the handle, which can come in handy when you have to measure what's being added. It's nice to have ladles of different sizes.

A normal-sized spatula is great for flipping eggs, but one with a longer base is great for anything that is so tender that it might break, such as fish or pancakes. When buying spatulas, look for ones with silicone, heat-tolerant ends; they are a little more expensive, but it is well worth the extra money. In fact, some of them are tolerant up to 700 degrees of heat.

Wooden spoons are great to use with aluminum pans because a stainless-steel spoon rubbing against an aluminum pan will turn a light-colored preparation grey. Wooden spoons also feel good in your hand.

When you buy stainless-steel spoons, make sure that you include in your collection a solid spoon, which is appropriate if you're trying to move sauce from a pan to a plate. In addition, you should have a slotted or perforated spoon

so that when you remove brussels sprouts from butter, for example, the butter can drain off before you move the food to the plate.

Some skimmers are appropriate for skimming stocks and sauces, and others—called spiders, which have an open net—are more appropriate for dipping foods out of hot oil. Because the net on spiders is open, the oil drains very quickly.

A food-grade brush is handy when you want to brush oil on top of food. It tolerates heat, so if it accidentally touches the pan, the bristles won't melt.

An ice cream scoop is great for ice cream, but it's also great when you're portioning muffins or small amounts of anything. Often, ice cream scoops are measured.

You can use kitchen shears for any cutting that goes on in the kitchen.

A meat mallet is great for pounding or tenderizing meat. If you don't have a meat mallet, however, you can also use a small saucepan to pound meat.

A nice selection of cookie sheets or sheet pans is handy to have in the kitchen.

A box grater, which is used to grate cheese or zest lemons, is a great kitchen tool. Many of them have different sizes of holes on each of the four sides of the grater.

A small digital thermometer is necessary when you are roasting food and need to take the temperature of the food, and a larger thermometer that has a probe can be put into a roast beef so that you can monitor its progress as it cooks.

You also need a selection of dishes that you can serve from, but those same dishes can be used to store food.

Graduated measuring cups are essential so that you can follow recipes with some confidence that the dishes will come out exactly the way they should if you are being accurate.

Tomato Concassé

If you simply chop up tomatoes and add them to a preparation like ratatouille, you will end up with both seeds and skins floating around in the pot. Instead, make tomato concassé, which is peeled, seeded, and coarsely chopped tomatoes.

First, take your knife and cut out the core of a few tomatoes, which can be discarded. Then, on the blossom end, cut a quick cross in the skin. Next, put the tomatoes in boiling water. If the tomatoes are very ripe, the skins begin to split where you cut the cross, and they begin to spread and peel away—usually within about 10 seconds. The riper the tomato is, the faster this will happen.

Mirepoix

A mirepoix is a collection of onions, celery, and carrots—50 percent onions and 25 percent of each of the other two. For lighter preparations, you can make a white mirepoix, which contains leeks, onions, celery, and parsnips.

Once the skin has loosened so that you can peel it off, take the tomatoes out of the boiling water and put them directly into ice water to keep the tomato pulp from cooking. After they have cooled enough, peel the skin off of the tomatoes with your hands.

Then, cut the tomatoes in half between the stem end and the blossom end; this opens up all of the little seed cavities so that you can gently squeeze the tomatoes and take the seeds out.

Finally, dice the tomatoes, using half-inch cuts. Cut each tomato horizontally in half and then into half-inch strips, turning it 90 degrees and cutting again.

This is a standard preparation of the French tradition. It might be worth having tomato concassé on hand in your kitchen so that you don't have to go through all of these steps every time you want to add tomatoes to a dish.

Ratatouille

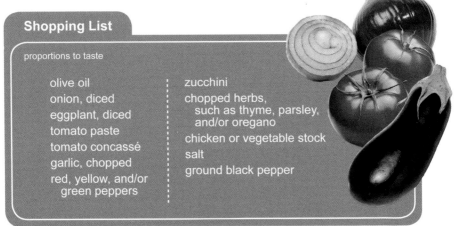

Shopping List

proportions to taste

olive oil
onion, diced
eggplant, diced
tomato paste
tomato concassé
garlic, chopped
red, yellow, and/or
green peppers

zucchini
chopped herbs,
    such as thyme, parsley,
    and/or oregano
chicken or vegetable stock
salt
ground black pepper

To make ratatouille, a simple vegetable stew, start by sautéing some onions in a pan that is on the heat. Dice an onion, making about quarter-inch slices. As soon as the pan is hot, add olive oil to it. Because onions have a very harsh, sulfurous quality, most recipes will start with the onions in the pan so that they can cook a little bit and lose some of that sulfurous quality—and pick up some sweetness in the process.

The next ingredient is eggplant, which should be diced before it is added to the pan. Allow it to sauté for a little while; eggplant needs to be fully cooked to taste good. One of the challenges with eggplant is that it's very thirsty, so you might have to add a little more oil for it to absorb.

Then, add some tomato paste to the pan and sauté it until it changes from a very bright red color to a brick red color. Make sure that nothing burns on the bottom of the pan. Finally, add tomato concassé and let the vegetables cook, turning the heat down just a little bit.

Add some garlic to the ratatouille. Crush it so that it's flat, and then chop it coarsely. As the ratatouille stews, the garlic will soften and melt away. You can also add some red, yellow, and/or green peppers and zucchini—which will also add some color. Add a few chopped herbs, such as thyme, parsley, and/

or oregano. Then, introduce a little bit of water—just enough water so that the vegetables can stew. You could use chicken or vegetable stock instead, but you can also just use the water that you used to make tomato concassé.

Put a lid on top of the pan, turn the temperature down very low, and simmer for about 20 minutes. Season with salt and pepper—and a little bit of fresh olive oil. Then, stir everything together. When you cook vegetables, you often want the vegetables to be cooked al dente, but in this case, you want them to be very tender.

Bouquet Garni

A bouquet garni is a bunch of thyme, celery, and parsley that is wrapped in a leek leaf and then tied with a piece of twine.

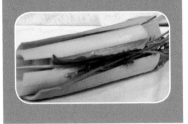

Clarified Butter

Clarified butter is a butter that has been melted so that it separates into its components: butterfat, buttermilk, and milk solids. Of those three, the butterfat tolerates heat very well, and the other two do not.

To make clarified butter, melt butter over a very low flame, and it will start to separate into its components. The milk solids float on top, and the buttermilk is on the bottom. Once the butter starts to separate, you can take a ladle and skim the milk solids off of the top. Then, continue to cook it over a very slow, gentle heat, and as it cooks, it will separate even more. Ultimately, the butter will be almost clear, and it will be pure fat.

The process of clarifying butter takes a few hours. Just let the butter simmer very gently on the stove, and a few hours later, it will have separated into clear fat—with the white foam on the top and the buttermilk below.

You can use clarified butter to fry an egg; the egg will move beautifully on the bottom of a nonstick pan and will not burn. You can even top your ratatouille with a fried egg to add protein to the dish.

Sachet d'Épices

A sachet d'épices is a little piece of cheesecloth made into a tea bag that has peppercorns, a bay leaf, thyme, parsley, and garlic.

Sauté—Dry-Heat Cooking with Fat

Lesson 4

In this lesson, you will learn about sautéing, which is a cooking technique that involves dry-heat cooking with fat. The significance of using oil, or fat, instead of water in this technique is that oil allows the use of very high temperatures, which allow your food to brown very effectively. Browned food not only looks great, but it also has great flavor. Steak, chicken, and fish are tender proteins that respond well to dry-heat cooking with fat, which is one of the four cooking techniques.

The Four Cooking Techniques

In all of cookery, there are only four cooking techniques: dry-heat cooking with fat, dry-heat cooking without fat, moist-heat cooking, and combination cooking. Dry-heat cooking with fat embraces sautéing and stir-frying. Dry-heat cooking without fat includes grilling, broiling, roasting, and baking. Moist-heat cooking involves poaching, steaming, simmering, and boiling. Combination cooking, as the name suggests, embraces more than one technique—such as braising and stewing, for example.

When you understand cooking as four basic techniques, then every time you practice a new recipe, you learn a little bit more about those techniques, and when you pick up a new recipe, you can understand it in the context of those four techniques. In other words, you don't have to start from scratch every time.

Chicken Marsala

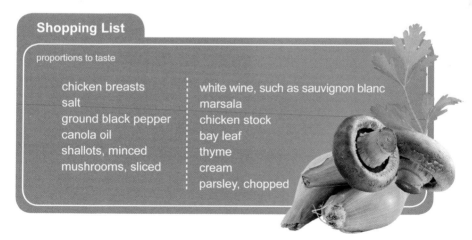

Shopping List

proportions to taste

chicken breasts	white wine, such as sauvignon blanc
salt	marsala
ground black pepper	chicken stock
canola oil	bay leaf
shallots, minced	thyme
mushrooms, sliced	cream
	parsley, chopped

The process of making chicken marsala utilizes sautéing, which is a type of dry-heat cooking with fat. Start by seasoning both sides of some chicken breasts with a little bit of salt and pepper. Make sure that you use a sauté pan that is on the larger side because if the pan is too small, then the chicken will not brown—instead, it will just simmer in its own liquid. Alternatively, if the pan is too large, then there will be portions of the pan that will not have food, and because there is nothing to absorb the excess heat, the oil is going to burn in those areas where there is no food.

Sautoir versus Sauteuse

A sautoir is a type of sauté pan that has straight sides while a sauteuse is a type of sauté pan that has curved sides. The straight sides of a sautoir are great for creating a sauce with a lot of liquid while the curved sides of a sauteuse are great for flipping food in a pan because the curved sides help the food jump back on itself.

Because sautéing is a high-heat technique, you want to begin with plenty of heat in the thermal mass of the pan. Therefore, start with the burner of the stove turned up all the way. Then, add any oil that has a high smoke point, such as canola oil, which is able to tolerate the high heat involved in sautéing. Once the oil begins to creep around the pan and you notice the first few wisps of smoke, the oil has reached its smoke point, so you want to add the chicken to the pan to bring the temperature down. When you put the chicken in the pan, make sure to put it in away from you so that you don't burn yourself.

If you ignore the first few wisps of smoke, the smoke point will quickly turn into the flash point. If you reach the flash point and your pan catches fire, put a lid on it, pull it off the heat, and the lid will starve the fire of oxygen. Then, you can just let the fire die out.

When you notice that some browning is beginning to take place, turn the temperature down just a little bit. As a general rule, cook chicken for eight minutes per inch of thickness, but regulate the heat so that the chicken doesn't brown too much too early in the process.

Once the sizzling in the pan starts to subside, you need to determine when it is appropriate to turn the chicken over so that the other side can cook. You want the browning on the first side to have progressed to the point where the fat has rendered out of the skin. Look for a nice golden color and then turn it over and cook it on the second side. When you stop hearing the sizzling once you have turned the chicken over, the chicken should be done cooking. The chicken should have a golden color on both sides, and the skin should be crispy.

Let the chicken rest in a warm spot while you make the sauce that will accompany the chicken. Allowing the chicken to rest for a little while will result in a juicier piece of meat because as the chicken cooked, pressure built up inside of the meat, and if you were to cut into it too quickly, that pressure would allow all the juices to flow out. As the chicken rests, the temperature and pressure begin to subside, and the juices remain where they should be.

Some of the liquid that is left in the pan after the chicken is done cooking is the fat, in the form of oil, that you started with, and some of it is the juices that came out of the chicken as it cooked. In order to separate the fat from the liquid so that you are left with just the chicken essence, put the pan back on the stove over heat and boil the liquid until it is dry. What's left will cling to the pan, and at that point, you can pour the excess fat out of the pan. Depending on how much moisture is in the liquid, this may take a minute or two, but don't let the liquid get so dark that it burns and becomes bitter.

> ## Which Foods Are Appropriate for Sautéing?
>
> Because sautéing is a high-heat cooking technique, you have to be careful what you cook using this method. There's nothing about high heat that will make food become more tender, so anything that is already tender—such as a chicken breast, steak, or piece of fish—would be appropriate for sautéing. If you tried to sauté something that is tough, such as a beef shank, it would brown, but it would not become tender.

The brown residue that is found on the bottom of the pan after you pour most of the fat out is called fond and will become the basis of the sauce that will accompany the chicken. To start, put the pan back on the heat and add some minced shallots and sliced mushrooms to it. As you sauté these vegetables, the sizzling that you hear is the moisture that is leaving them. When the fond seems like it is getting too dark, deglaze the pan by introducing a little bit of white wine, such as sauvignon blanc. Then, add some marsala, which is a sweet wine. The addition of the wine will bring the temperature of the pan down. Use some tongs to scrape the residue off the bottom of the pan. This should taste rich, savory, and a little acidic because of the wine.

When Is Chicken Done Cooking?

There are a number of ways to determine doneness for a chicken breast. For chicken that is thin, it is easiest to just poke it with your finger, making sure to test it in the thickest part of the meat. The way to understand what you feel is as follows: If you relax your hand and poke yourself in the thick part of your palm, it should feel like raw meat. If you touch your thumb to your first finger, the thick part of your palm will firm up, and that is what rare meat should feel like. If you touch your thumb to your middle finger and then poke that same part of your palm, that is what medium meat should feel like. If you do the same thing with your ring finger, it will feel like medium-well meat, and if you do the same thing with your pinky, it will feel like well-done meat.

Let the liquid in the pan simmer, reducing it until it is nearly dry—what the French would call à sec. If you decide you want a larger amount of sauce, you can also introduce some chicken stock, which reinforces the flavor of chicken as it reduces. While the liquid simmers, add a bay leaf and a branch of thyme, just to make the flavor more complex.

As soon as the pan is almost dry, add some cream to it. You need enough sauce for all of the chicken breasts you cooked, but don't be too generous because if you add too much cream, it will water down the flavor of the sauce. As this liquid reduces even further, it will start to thicken.

Once the sauce is done, you can turn down the heat and place the chicken into the pan with the sauce—just to warm it up very briefly. The sauce should be fairly assertive because it has to flavor the entire dish, so it may need to be more assertive than you would expect it to taste on its own. You want the sauce to coat the back of a spoon while still being a liquid— which is referred to in French as nappé. Season the sauce with salt and pepper, swirling each in. Then, remove the bay leaf and thyme. Finally, put the chicken—

along with some sauce—on a plate and put a little bit of chopped parsley on top to add some color to this dish.

Chicken Paillard with Warm Salad

Shopping List

proportions to taste

chicken breasts	arugula
salt	radicchio
ground black pepper	Belgian endive
olive oil	cherry tomatoes
chicken stock	toasted or grilled bread
lemon juice	

To make this rustic sauté, start with some chicken breasts, removing the skin and trimming the fat. Next, you are going to turn the chicken breasts into what is known in France as a paillard, which is a piece of meat that has been pounded into what resembles a thin straw mat. This process makes a tougher cut of meat tender, but you can also use this technique on meat that is already tender to make it thinner so that it cooks faster. Place the chicken in a ziplock bag and gently pound it with a mallet, making sure that the chicken breasts become uniformly thick. If you don't have a mallet, you can use a pot or pan instead.

Once the chicken breasts are about a quarter of the thickness they were—which will allow them to cook four times faster—turn the heat up on a pan and season both sides of the chicken with salt and a lot of pepper. Then, add olive oil, which has a high smoke point, to the pan. Once you see the first few wisps of smoke, put the chicken in the pan away from yourself with its presentation side down. While the chicken begins to cook, wash everything that had raw chicken on it, including your hands.

Because the chicken is thin, the temperature of the pan can be a little bit on the hotter side, which also means that it won't be in the pan for as long. When a pan is really hot, you will find that almost nothing will stick to it; it's only when you put food into a pan that is a little bit cool that you can run into problems with sticking.

In the case of chicken, you always want it to be cooked until it is well done, and you want both sides of the chicken to look nice and golden—not burnt or

too crusty. As soon as it is done cooking, remove the chicken from the pan and let it rest.

After you remove the chicken from the pan, you should see the brown fond that developed on the bottom of the pan. Deglaze the pan with chicken stock, reducing it until it is almost dry, to reinforce the chicken flavor of the paillard. Make sure there is no brown fond stuck to the bottom of the pan.

The Presentation Side

When a pan is hot and you add food to it, you should add the food on the side that you would consider to be the presentation side, which is the most attractive side. Basically, you want the side that will be facing up when you give it to guests to go into the pan when the pan is clean so that it continues to be the best-looking side.

Once the liquid is reduced, add some acid to it in the form of lemon juice. Then, season the sauce with a little bit of salt and pepper. Finally, add olive oil as if you were making a vinaigrette dressing. The preferred ratio for a vinaigrette dressing is one part acid to three parts oil, but because you also have the chicken glaze, use slightly less oil than three parts. You want the sauce to be too sharp, too salty, and too peppery—with the understanding that it will be less assertive on top of the chicken.

Next, prepare an arugula, radicchio, and Belgian endive salad with some cherry tomatoes. Season the salad with some salt and pepper. The sauce that was made from the chicken essence will also be used as the dressing for this salad. When you are ready to serve this dish, use the warm vinaigrette to dress the greens, tossing all of the components of the salad together. The way to evaluate a vinaigrette is to taste it on the salad that it accompanies.

Then, put the chicken on top of the greens and sprinkle some extra cherry tomatoes on top. Finally, top the chicken with just a little bit of sauce to make everything glisten and taste great. The only thing missing is some sort of starch, which could be toasted or grilled bread.

Browning Reactions

Browning is a high-heat cooking technique that reaches temperatures above 300 degrees. In those temperature ranges, some browning reactions take place. For example, caramelization, in which sugars begin to brown, happens at about 300 to 310 degrees. In addition, the Maillard reaction takes place between proteins and carbohydrates, and while it begins at about 250 degrees, it is in full form at above 300 degrees. The Maillard reaction not only offers the brown color that develops, but it also results in hundreds of flavor and aroma compounds. In general, browning translates into flavor.

Roasting—Dry-Heat Cooking without Fat
Lesson 5

R oasting is a dry-heat cooking method without fat. The circulating air in the oven chamber is actually what does the cooking. Air is not a great conductor of heat, so roasting is a gentler cooking technique. There are many benefits to roasting, but perhaps the best is that it seems like there are always leftovers on hand for a sandwich or a roast beef hash. There are also the benefits of the warmth of the oven and the captivating aroma in the house that develops as you are roasting.

The Equipment

If your oven smokes when you preheat it, you must clean it before you begin. If smoke builds up in your oven, it will flavor the food that you are roasting.

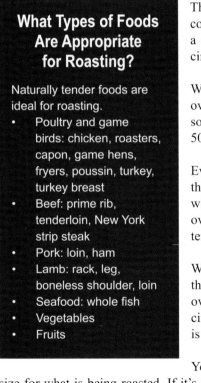

What Types of Foods Are Appropriate for Roasting?

Naturally tender foods are ideal for roasting.
- Poultry and game birds: chicken, roasters, capon, game hens, fryers, poussin, turkey, turkey breast
- Beef: prime rib, tenderloin, New York strip steak
- Pork: loin, ham
- Lamb: rack, leg, boneless shoulder, loin
- Seafood: whole fish
- Vegetables
- Fruits

There are two types of ovens: a conventional oven, which has no fan, and a convection oven, which has a fan that circulates the air inside the oven.

When the air circulates in a convection oven, the cooking becomes more efficient, so you can turn the oven down 25 to 50 degrees.

Every oven has a thermometer in it, but there's no guarantee that the thermometer will be accurate. Therefore, buy a small oven thermometer as insurance that the temperature is what you expect it to be.

When roasting, place the oven rack in the middle or in the bottom third of the oven so that the hot air of the oven can be circulated all the way around the food that is being roasted.

You need a pan that's the appropriate size for what is being roasted. If it's too large, portions of the pan will burn. If it's too small, air can't circulate around the food. Cast-iron pans are great for roasting.

How to Truss a Chicken

In order to avoid burning the wing tips and legs of your chicken while it is roasting, take the wings and fold them under the body of the chicken and then pull the legs in tight to the breast.

Place the middle of a piece of string that is about five feet long under the bird on either side of the legs. Bring the strings up and cross the legs, capturing them tightly.

Then, take the string on the left, cross it over to the right, and run it between the breast and the leg. In addition, take the string on the right, cross it over to the left, and run it between the breast and the leg.

Once you have captured both of the wings, bring the string under the neck and then tie the string and cut it off. A trussed bird roasts as one entire unit rather than as two flopped-out legs and two flopped-out wings.

Roasted Chicken with Roasted Potatoes

Before you put any food in the oven, it's important to get everything prepped and seasoned. To roast the potatoes, start by preheating the oven to 450 degrees. At this temperature, the potatoes will take about 35 to 40 minutes.

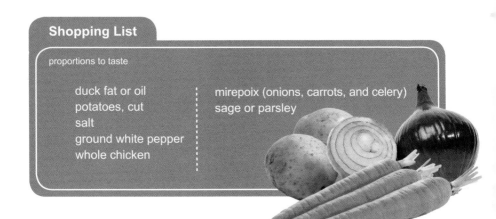
Heat the pan, adding a little bit of duck fat. If you don't have any, regular oil is fine. Once the pan is hot and the fat or oil is just beginning to smoke, add some cut potatoes—in just one layer. Then, they are ready to go into the oven. The potatoes are done when they are a nice golden brown and are tender if you pierce them with a knife. Take the potatoes out of the pan, removing them from the fat, and keep them warm until you are ready to serve the chicken. Add a little bit of salt and pepper.

Season both the inside and outside of the chicken with salt and pepper. At 450 degrees, the chicken will brown very quickly. Leave it at that temperature for about 15 minutes, and then turn it down to about 350 degrees, allowing it to roast until it is fully cooked. If you leave the temperature too high, the heat is too aggressive and will dry the bird out.

Once the chicken is browned, turn the oven down and add a selection of vegetables—such as onions, carrots, and celery—to the roasting pan. These vegetables, often called a mirepoix, will roast along with the chicken drippings that are collecting in the pan and will lend flavor to what is going to become the gravy.

Once the chicken is done, remove the trussing. Cut the twine that you trussed it with in only one place so that you know that you got all of the parts of the string off. If you cut the twine in more than one place, sometimes a little bit is left behind.

Move the chicken over to a platter. Strain the sauce that is left in the roasting pan and set it aside. Make sure that you get all of the goodness out of the vegetables by pressing on them slightly. Add a little bit of salt and pepper to the sauce. You can also chop up a few leaves of sage or parsley and add them to the sauce.

Making Gravy from a Roast

Gravy is nothing more than a sauce that is made from the pan drippings of a roast—whether it is a beef roast or a roasted chicken. After removing the chicken from the oven, in the bottom of the roasting pan is the mirepoix that you added that has had a chance to cook and flavor the juices that have come from that chicken.

Turn the temperature of the oven up a little bit. There's a certain amount of water in the chicken's juices, and if you cook it over high heat, the water will boil away, and the essence of the chicken and the vegetables will remain.

Once the water has boiled away, all of the juice will cling to the pan, and you can pour the excess fat off. As long as you hear sizzling, there's probably a little water left. At no point do you want to see the bottom of the pan burning. If it's burning, you're destroying your sauce. Once the fat starts to become clear, it means that the water has cooked out of it.

How to Determine Doneness

The most dependable method of determining when a chicken is fully cooked in the oven is to use a thermometer. Put the thermometer into the thickest part of the meat and take the internal temperature of that meat. You are aiming for an internal temperature of 165 degrees Fahrenheit. At that temperature, you no longer have to worry about salmonella, and at the same time, the meat will still be juicy and moist.

Set the fat aside. To thicken the hot fat, mix some flour into it and cook the flour in the hot fat until it loses its raw flavor—which will take about 10 to 15 minutes. To keep it from sticking to the bottom of the pan, keep stirring it. You have just made a roux.

Once the roux is made, add some chicken stock. You will notice that as the chicken stock comes up to a boil, it will thicken almost immediately because the starch granules in the flour expand as they absorb the liquid. Because you worked hard to get a nice, crispy, golden crust on the chicken, serve the gravy on the side of the roasted chicken.

Carving a Roasted Chicken

Place the chicken on a cutting board. Pull the leg away from the breast and cut the skin between the breast and the leg. As you open the area between the breast and the leg, follow the seam between the breast and the leg, and then you'll see the hip joint. If you pull the leg back far enough, it will come off. Then, cut through the skin to detach the leg from the body. Do the same on the other side. Then, cut each leg in half.

Flip the chicken over and cut between the drumstick and the thigh. In every joint, there is a little sweet spot where the knife will slide right through. Then, you are left with the rest of the carcass. Cut both wings off, using the same method of cutting.

Next, you have the two breasts, which are separated by the sternum. On a chicken, this is called a keel bone. Cut on either side of the keel bone, pushing the meat off the carcass. The wishbone will be at the end; just cut through the wishbone (which would be the collarbone on a person). Follow the rib cage around, and pull off the entire breast.

The shoulder joint, like all the other joints, has a sweet spot. Follow the keel bone until you reach the rib cage and then follow the rib cage around, pulling the breast meat off. Once you get down to the shoulder joint, cut through the skin to reach the other breast. Each breast is a large portion, so each one should be cut into a few separate pieces.

The leftover carcass is the basis for a really delicious stock, which could then become a soup. Don't throw the carcass away. Either simmer it or throw it into the freezer. If you put it in the freezer, you can retrieve it later and simmer it.

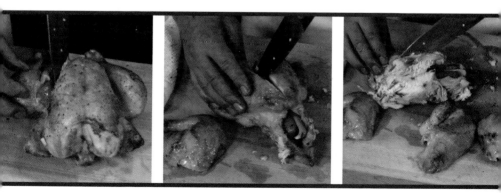

Frying—Dry-Heat Cooking with Fat

Lesson 6

In this lesson, you are going to learn how to cook some of the world's favorite dishes. This is a lesson on frying, which is a dry-heat cooking technique with fat. Sautéing is a similar technique, but the difference is that frying—both pan-frying and deep fat frying—uses a large amount of oil while sautéing uses a small amount of oil.

Pan-Fried Veal Cutlet

Shopping List

proportions to taste

boneless veal top round	water
salt	dried bread crumbs
ground black pepper	canola oil
all-purpose flour	parsley, coarsely cut
eggs, beaten	lemon juice

Kitchen Safety

If you put a pan of oil on the heat, don't leave it unattended in the kitchen. If you do, the temperature of the oil will rise, and it will reach the smoke point. If you're not there to turn it down, you'll find yourself at the flash point, where it bursts spontaneously into flame. If you do have a fire, turn the burner off, take a lid, and put it on top of the fire. That will starve the fire of oxygen and will put the fire out.

Pan-frying is a high-heat cooking technique that uses a shallow pan. Just like when you sauté, you need to begin with tender foods because the high heat involved will not make food tender.

To make a piece of veal tender, pound it in order to break the fibers and make it thin and broad. Lay it on a piece of parchment paper, and with a knife, butterfly it open and then put another piece of parchment paper on top of it. Then, use a kitchen mallet to pound it.

Once your meat is tender, season it with a little bit of salt and pepper on both sides. Then, use a standard breading. This involves coating both sides of the meat with flour, patting off the excess. Then, dip it in a mixture containing beaten eggs and a little bit of water and, finally, in dried bread crumbs. This standard breading will coat your piece of meat, which on its own doesn't have a tremendous amount of flavor, and it will protect the meat from the heat of the oil. It will also protect the oil from the moisture—which holds the juices and flavor—in the meat.

Then, your meat is ready to be cooked. Start by adding canola oil, which has a relatively high smoke point, to a pan that is already heated up on the stove. Use enough oil so that it fills about a third of the pan. Any more than that, and you will run the risk of the oil spilling over the top of the veal cutlet, soaking the bread crumbs on top and making it a little bit oily.

Frying Tips

A countertop deep fat fryer is best for frying, but many people do not have one at home. Instead, you can use a pan filled halfway with oil. Don't ever fill a pot that you're frying in any fuller than halfway because as you fry, the oil will seethe up. When frying, you need a place to drain things that have been fried. You also need some common kitchen tools to manipulate the food once it is in the fat. If your stove has a hood, which draws air up and away, make sure that it's turned on.

To evaluate the temperature of the oil, take a few bread crumbs and throw them in the pan. If they sizzle right away, that means that the temperature is at least 212 degrees. If they brown within about a minute, then the temperature is closer to 350 degrees, which is what you want the temperature to be. If you see smoke coming off of the pan, then you know that you've reached the smoke point of that oil, so you should turn the temperature down. At that point, you can also just add the food, which will bring the temperature down.

For a piece of meat that is about a quarter to a half of an inch thick, cook each side for about two minutes. When you start to notice a golden color on the first side, flip it over. Once the pan has recovered the initial loss of temperature from the addition of the meat, you can turn the heat down a little bit, but listen for the sizzle that tells you that the pan is hot.

When the meat has finished cooking, the bread will have absorbed a little bit of oil—but not too much. The moisture in the bread will actually force the fat away from this product and not really absorb it. Remove the pan from the heat; otherwise, the fat will continue to cook. Turn the burner off, and allow the meat to sit for just a second so that the fat can drain off of it.

Because your veal cutlet has a crusty, golden exterior, it would be a mistake to top it with a wet sauce because it would become soggy. Instead, use a simple garnish. For example, wrap some capers in anchovy fillets. In addition, you can cut some parsley leaves very coarsely and sprinkle those on top. Finally, squeeze a little bit of lemon on at the last possible minute so that the veal stays nice and crispy.

Fish and Chips with Beer Batter

Shopping List

proportions to taste

potatoes, cut	**Beer Batter for Fish**
canola oil	all-purpose flour
salt	salt
fish, such as lingcod, cut	baking powder
	egg, separated into yolk and white
	beer

Start by washing some of the surface starch off of the outside of your potatoes so that they will brown nicely. Cut them up and sort of square them off, but don't make them look too perfect. Put them into a pot of water right away so that they don't discolor.

The potatoes can be stored in water overnight if you like. Once they have been soaked, remove them from the water and blot them dry because if you add water into hot fat, you get sort of an explosive reaction.

Because raw potatoes are not very tender, if you were to put them into hot fat as they are, they would brown before they became tender. Therefore, cook them in a two-stage method. First, cook them in a pan of canola oil (filled halfway) at a lower temperature, around 300 degrees, and allow them to get tender all the way through. To determine tenderness, take the potatoes out of the oil and shake them; they should rustle a little bit. You can also take one out, drain it, break it open, and taste it. This probably takes about one to one and a half minutes.

Checking Tenderness of Meat

If you want to evaluate your meat to see if it's actually tender, you can take your thumb and forefinger and press on it, and if you can press your fingers through the meat, then it's tender enough to progress.

Once the potatoes are tender, take them out of the oil and drain them on an absorbent towel. At this point, they won't discolor anymore because the enzymes that make them turn color will have all been destroyed by the heat. Then, turn up the heat on the oil—from 300 up to about 375 degrees—and cook the potatoes in the pan until they are brown, golden, and crisp. While they're still hot and a little bit wet with oil, season them with salt. Set them aside and keep them warm until you fry the fish.

The Basket Method of Frying

Restaurants usually use the basket method of frying, which involves using a basket to deep-fry many different types of food. A basket is a problem if you want to fry something that is too large for the basket or if you have something dipped in batter because the batter can adhere itself to the basket.

Start to finish, this method of frying, which is known as the swimming method, involves about one and a half minutes of blanching at a lower temperature—around 300 degrees—and another one and a half minutes of final cooking at a temperature of around 375 degrees.

To make the beer batter, stir together all-purpose flour, about a half of a teaspoon of salt, and about a quarter of a teaspoon of baking powder. Then, add an egg yolk, but set the white aside. Make sure that none of the yolk gets into the white because you're going to whip the white until it is nice and frothy, and any yolk, which is fat, will be a problem.

Little by little, add cold beer to the flour mixture. Start by breaking up the egg yolk, and as you add more beer, drag more and more of the flour into the mix. Break up any lumps as you go, but don't overmix because it will become too glutinous and tough.

Set the mixture aside for about 30 to 45 minutes so that the gluten in the flour can begin to relax and become much more tender. Then, whip the egg white, which will probably quadruple in volume, until it is nice and frothy and add it to the batter.

The Nature of Fat

Because you spent some time whipping air into the egg white, it's important not to stir all that air out. Therefore, gently fold the whipped egg white into the batter until it is homogenous. Try not to overmanipulate the mixture. Your beer batter is now ready.

Every fat has its own smoke point, which is where it begins to break down. When you are frying, it is important to use a fat that is stable and resists high temperature over time. Heat is one of a few different things that will make fat break down. When frying, you want to keep the heat under control, but you also want to choose an oil that has a tolerance for heat, such as cottonseed oil, peanut oil, canola oil, and even low-grade olive oil.

When ready to fry, choose a fish like lingcod and cut it into pieces that are not too large. If the pieces are too large, they will take too long to cook in such hot oil and will burn on the outside before they cook all the way through. Also, the fish should not be too wet.

Completely coat the fish in the beer batter, being careful to let the excess drip off, and then ease it into the hot oil, which should be at about 375 degrees. Also be careful not to dip your fingers into the hot oil. You may discover that you need to turn the fish every now and then. If there is one side that is pale, it just needs to be turned. When the fish is done, take it out of the pan. Don't forget to turn off your stove.

Serve your fish and chips in a basket with a piece of paper in the bottom. Traditionally, you would use newspaper. Stack the french fries in the bottom of the basket, and tuck a little bit of dipping sauce in the bottom as well. Then, stack the fried fish on top of the french fries. Season with any herbs or spices that you want to add.

Fried Parsnips

Shopping List

proportions to taste

parsnips, peeled
   and thinly sliced
oil
salt

ground black pepper
parmesan cheese,
   thinly shaved
parsley

When Are the Parsnips Done?

When you put parsnips into a hot pan, they will bubble, which tells you that there is a lot of water inherent in that vegetable and that the water in that vegetable is boiling. As long as the parsnips are bubbling, there is still moisture in them. If you were to take them out of the pan while they are still bubbling—even if they had browned—they would be soggy and limp. However, if you notice that the bubbling begins to subside and then they begin to brown, you can be relatively confident that when you take them out and they cool, they'll be crisp.

When it comes to frying, parsnips are a problem because they contain so much sugar that if you were to fry them at 375 degrees, they would burn long before they ever became crispy and crunchy.

Peel and thinly slice some parsnips in such a way that the pieces are uniform and not falling apart. Gather the slices and add them to a pan that contains oil and is at a temperature of around 300 degrees. Separate them in the pan so that they can fry evenly and don't stick together. Depending on how much you are frying, this could take 5 to 10 minutes.

If you make the mistake of not cutting the parsnip pieces evenly and you have some that are thick and some that are thin, you can expect that some will begin to brown first and others will take a little bit longer to brown. In that case, you may have to remove those that are already brown from the oil.

Transfer any parsnip pieces that are done cooking to a bowl or pan so that they can drain. You will know when they are done because they will stop bubbling in the pan. After you remove them, when they're still hot and a little bit oily from the fat, season them with salt and pepper, which will cling to the outside.

Make sure you turn the heat off underneath the oil before you leave the kitchen, and if the oil you used is clean, you can strain it, put it in your refrigerator, and use it again.

If you are going to serve these as a bar snack, try introducing some savory flavors to these sweet parsnip pieces. Thinly shave some parmesan cheese, and mix the shards of cheese in with the parsnips. Just so it pops on a plate, put some parsley on top.

A Warning about Fat

If you cook with fat for too long, it can begin to break down. You won't be able to get it up to the requisite temperature without it starting to smoke. It will also get dark, which is typically an indication that it is starting to become ruined. Finally, over time, it will start to turn rancid—a quality that has a very distinctive and unpleasant smell.

From Poach to Steam—
Moist-Heat Cooking
Lesson 7

The focus of this lesson is on moist-heat cooking methods. The world is covered with water, and most of the vegetables and foods that we eat are comprised primarily of water. For example, a head of lettuce is more than 90 percent water, and even our bodies contain about 70 percent water. Liquid is all around us, and moist-heat cooking is all about finessing the application of heat to liquid.

Moist-Heat Cooking

Freezing, poaching, simmering, boiling, steaming, and even pressure-cooking are all moist-heat cooking techniques that represent the application of heat to liquid in varying degrees of temperature.

Freezing is the absence of temperature; freezing takes heat away until a liquid turns to a solid. Poaching takes place at a much higher temperature—around 160 degrees. Simmering takes place at around 185 degrees. Boiling occurs at 212 degrees; more energy needs to be added to boiling water to get it to change into a vapor, or steam. Therefore, there is more energy available to cook in steaming than in poaching or boiling. Finally, pressure-cooking takes advantage of raising atmospheric pressure so that a few more degrees of temperature can be eked out.

Poaching with Tender Foods

The foods that are appropriate for poaching are foods that are already naturally tender. There is nothing about the delicate heat of poaching that will make tough foods tender. For example, you can't poach a beef shank or a tough piece of chuck. Chicken breast, shrimp, and salmon are great choices, however.

Poaching comes in two very broad categories: deep poaching, which involves poaching a food that is completely submerged in liquid, and shallow poaching, in which you use less liquid—and that liquid becomes the basis for a sauce.

Salmon with *Salsa Verde*

This dish utilizes the deep-poaching method. Because deep poaching involves a lot of liquid, you need to use a sautoir pan, which has straight sides and is fairly deep. Start by obtaining a piece of salmon that has been cut in half. Cut some portions of the salmon so that you can poach it. Cut some thinner pieces as well so that hopefully you get some that are properly cooked, some that are overcooked, and some that are maybe a little bit undercooked.

Cook the salmon in a court bouillon, which is nothing more than a vegetable stock that has the addition of a little bit of acidity and some herbs. You're going to cook the salmon in a liquid, so you don't want to put seasonings on the salmon itself because the liquid will wash away the seasonings on the salmon. Instead, you want to add the salmon to liquid that has already been seasoned so that it lends its flavor to the fish.

Grab some herbs—such as parsley, thyme, and a bay leaf—and wrap them with a strip of lemon zest, tying all of the herbs into a little bundle. This bundle, called a bouquet garni, is not unlike a sachet d'épices. Add the bouquet garni to the court bouillon.

The acidity is going to come in the form of some lemon juice and a little bit of wine. Taste the flavor of the bouillon, and season it with a little bit of salt and pepper.

Deep poaching is a delicate cooking technique, so you need to make sure that the temperature of the bouillon is just right before adding the salmon. Use a thermometer to make sure that it reaches about 160 degrees, and then add the salmon to the pan. When you put the fish in the pan, its surface will begin to darken and turn opaque.

Even if you don't have a thermometer, there are a few clues to knowing when the bouillon is ready. First, you should not see bubbles breaking in the poaching

liquid or forming on the bottom of the pan. If you do, then you're probably at a minimum of 180 to 185 degrees, which is classified as a simmer. Second, at about 160 degrees, you'll just begin to see a little bit of steam coming off of the bottom of the liquid in the pan. At about 140 degrees, you will notice a convection action that begins to take place in the bottom of the pan. You will see some of the spices you added rising from the bottom of the pan and then floating to the top. Then, they will cool and sink back down to the bottom of the pan.

Chopping Full-Flavored Foods

If you are chopping foods that are full of flavor, such as garlic and anchovies, if you chop them with parsley, the flavor of the full-flavored ingredients makes its way into the parsley and doesn't get smeared all over your cutting board.

As soon as you add the fish to the bouillon, the temperature will probably drop about 10 degrees because the fish was at room temperature before you added it. Then, the temperature has to recover. If you see little beads of white protein coming out of the fish and beginning to form on the surface of the water, then that is indicative of a temperature that is too high, so you need to turn it down. Those little beads of white protein are called albumin, which is also found in egg whites.

After about 8 to 10 minutes per inch of thickness, check on the pieces of salmon. Give them a little squeeze to determine if the inside is done cooking; if you break into a piece, the tender flesh should be cooked gently all the way to the center. The salmon should be moist and should flake easily.

When any of the pieces are ready to come out of the pan, gently blot them dry and put them onto a plate with an absorbent towel, which will absorb all of the excess liquid. You can use a skimmer, which supports the fish so that it doesn't break. Remember that you want some of the pieces to overcook and some to undercook.

While the salmon is poaching, make a sauce called *salsa verde*, which is a green herb sauce. Start with parsley, a few anchovy fillets, and some capers. Mash a clove of garlic and add it to the parsley mixture. Then, chop it all up.

Then, transfer those ingredients into a bowl, adding some olive oil and lemon juice to moisten it. Season it with a little bit of salt and pepper—and even some pepper flakes if you want it to be spicy. It should be assertive because it has to flavor all of the fish that you have poached.

Because the process of poaching doesn't give much flavor, a difference in texture, or a bright color, the *salsa verde* is an integral part of this dish. Serve it on top of the salmon to complement its pale appearance. You might also want to serve the salmon with a lemon wedge when you plate it.

Taste the salmon with the sauce you just made. The fish is about richness and texture while the sauce is about depth of flavor. There's a lot of acidity and salt in the sauce from the capers and anchovies, and the two should taste great together.

Any sort of tender fish like salmon would be appropriate for this dish. In addition, the sauce is a vinaigrette-based sauce, but you could also use a mayonnaise-based sauce instead.

Monkfish Provençal

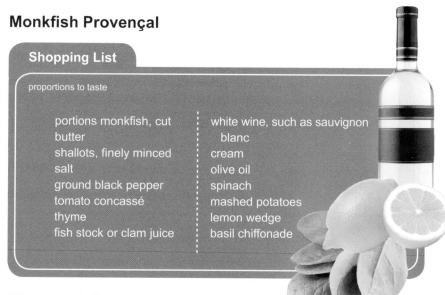

Shopping List

proportions to taste

portions monkfish, cut	white wine, such as sauvignon
butter	blanc
shallots, finely minced	cream
salt	olive oil
ground black pepper	spinach
tomato concassé	mashed potatoes
thyme	lemon wedge
fish stock or clam juice	basil chiffonade

When you shallow poach a fish, such as monkfish, the poaching liquid becomes the basis for the sauce that accompanies the fish. On the other hand, you almost never use the court bouillon after you're done deep poaching a fish. Remember that shallow poaching also uses less liquid than deep poaching.

After your fish has been cleaned and is ready for cooking, coat the bottom of a sauteuse pan, a pan with sloped sides, with butter so that the fish does not stick to the pan. Because you will be using less liquid than when you deep poached salmon, a smaller pan is appropriate.

Sprinkle the bottom of the pan with shallots, an aromatic vegetable, that have been very finely minced. This will hold the fish up from the bottom of the pan and help prevent it from sticking. Shallots have a powerful onion flavor, but they are much smaller than an onion, so it's a lot easier to make the pieces small when mincing.

Then, cut the fish into a few pieces and add them to the pan—with the presentation side, or nicest side, of each fish up. One of the challenges with poaching is that there is no browning and no variance in texture because the temperature is very gentle and mild, so it is best to add some seasoning, such as salt and pepper. To add some color to the fish, top each piece of fish with what is known as tomato concassé, which is peeled, seeded, and diced tomatoes. This will flavor the fish as it cooks and will also give the fish some variation in texture. You can also add some thyme.

Monkfish: What's in a Name?

Monkfish takes its name from the fact that it looks like it has a huge hood over its head. Monkfish is also sometimes called "poor man's lobster" because the texture of monkfish tail meat is similar to the tail meat of lobster.

To create the poaching liquid, add 50 percent fish stock and 50 percent white wine to the pan. If you don't have fish stock, you can use canned clam juice. In addition, make sure to use a wine that has a backbone of acidity, such as sauvignon blanc, that will lend structure to the dish and will cut through any fishiness. Do not use a sweet wine.

The liquid should fill about a third to a half of the pan. You need to have enough sauce for all of your portions of monkfish. If you don't have enough liquid, then a portion of fish will not get any sauce, and if you add too much liquid, the sauce will lack depth and will be watered down.

You need a tight-fitting lid for your pan. If you don't have one, you can create what the French call a cartouche, which is simply a piece of parchment paper that is folded several times to fit the size of the pan and that has a small vent in the middle. This folded paper will hold the steam or moisture in place. Then, you can place a lid over the pan if you have one. If not, then use a piece of foil to seal the cartouche tightly.

The temperature of the pan should be exactly the same as the temperature for deep poaching—about 160 degrees. If the fish starts to simmer, the temperature is probably at about 185 degrees, so you need to turn the heat down. The fish will take about eight minutes per inch of thickness to fully cook.

To determine doneness, give the monkfish a squeeze; it should feel firm all the way through. You also might want to cut into a piece. Monkfish doesn't flake quite as readily as other fish, so cutting into it is less of an indicator of doneness. Keep the fish warm by placing the cartouche on top of it.

The next step for this preparation is to turn up the heat to the highest possible heat setting because the poaching liquid—which is referred to as *cuisson* by the French—

Garniture versus Garnish

If you add something to a dish, such as the tomato and thyme on top of the monkfish, and it becomes an integral part of the dish, then that is a garniture. On the other hand, a garnish is something that can be used in the dish but really is separate from the dish, such as a small piece of parsley or a wedge of lemon.

needs to be reduced. You can now taste the liquid; no raw fish is in it anymore. You will taste the acid from the wine and the richness not just of the fish stock, but also of the fish, tomatoes, and thyme.

To reduce the liquid, you need to cook the water out of it until you have a flavor concentrate, which will be the basis of the sauce. While you wait for the liquid to reduce, heat up a sauté pan and add some olive oil and spinach. In addition to the thyme-and-tomato topping that is on the fish, the spinach is another vegetable that will go along with the fish. Spinach doesn't take long to cook; you will barely have enough time to season it before it's done.

After about 10 minutes, the *cuisson* should be reduced to being nearly dry. If you taste it, you will find that it is concentrated—maybe even overconcentrated—which is how it should be. However, it is slightly thin, so it needs some cream to thicken it. Add cream and reduce the liquid again. This will become the sauce. The cream will reduce by about 40 percent, and the *cuisson* will become thicker.

Basil Chiffonade

As an herb that is delicious with tomatoes, basil is often used in Provençal cooking. However, as soon as you cut it, it will start to turn brown. Therefore, it can't be chopped in the way that you would chop parsley. Instead, you can use a technique called chiffonade, which involves stacking the basil leaves on top of each other, rolling them up into what look like little cigars, and then cutting them into small ribbons with a sharp knife. This is perhaps the least invasive way of cutting basil so that it holds onto its green color and doesn't turn black because its enzymes are suddenly exposed to the air.

Because you want the water vapor to escape, don't put the lid back on the sauteuse after you add the cream. In addition, cream has the annoying habit of boiling over, so when you see it start to boil, keep your eye on it and make sure that the heat doesn't need to be turned down.

Toward the end of the reduction process, put the fish back into the sauce very briefly to warm it—along with any poaching liquid that might have collected on the plate that it was sitting on.

Evaluate the sauce one last time; it should coat the back of a spoon very nicely. If it tastes good, you can turn the heat off. Sauces should taste a little saltier than you're comfortable with tasting off of a spoon, so add some salt if needed.

Finally, put some mashed potatoes on a plate and lay the spinach across them. Then, lay the fish on top, along with the tomato topping, and garnish with a lemon wedge and a branch of thyme. Mask the fish with some of the sauce, making sure that the potatoes and spinach get some sauce as well. Sprinkle the top with basil.

Braising and Stewing—
Combination Cooking

A s the name suggests, combination cooking involves combining more than one cooking technique; specifically, in this lesson, it involves combining dry-heat cooking with fat and moist-heat cooking in the forms of braising and stewing. Braising is typically reserved for larger cuts of tough meat—either portion sized or multi-portion sized. Stewing, on the other hand, is typically reserved for bite-sized pieces of meat. Stewing also requires more liquid than braising. Beyond these two differences, the techniques are almost interchangeable.

Braised Chuck Roast and Vegetables

Shopping List

proportions to taste

beef shoulder, trimmed	veal stock and chicken stock
canola oil	pearl onions, cut large
onions, diced	baby turnips, cut large
tomato paste	new potatoes, cut large
dry red wine	baby carrots, cut large
sachet d'épices (parsley, a bay leaf, peppercorns, thyme, and a clove of garlic)	salt
	ground black pepper

Start by heating a pan on the stove. For braising, use a large cut of tough meat, such as chuck, which is the shoulder of the animal. There will be a lot of connective tissue, fat, and even some bones.

If you were just to sauté this piece of meat, it would end up tough, but because you are going to be braising it, all of these parts of the animal will give some type of flavor or texture. Above about 160 degrees, the connective tissue begins to melt into gelatin and gives you a wonderful mouthfeel. The fat makes the meat rich, and the bones give the same flavor that they give in a stock.

As the first step of braising, brown the piece of meat. The Maillard reaction is responsible for the process of browning. To brown the meat, start by adding vegetable oil to a sauté pan that can withstand high heat. When you see the first few wisps of smoke coming off of the pan, you can add the meat to the pan. If you are using a large cut of meat, be careful to place it in the pan away from yourself.

Cook the piece of meat for about five minutes on the first side. Then, flip it over. Don't allow it to cook so hot that the pan burns because what develops in the pan will be the basis of the liquid that the meat will braise in. When you lift the piece of meat up from the pan, you should be able to see the fond that is beginning to develop in the bottom. Once the meat has been properly browned, remove it from the pan.

Next, introduce some aromatic onions to the pan and cook them until they're brown and caramelized, which will take only a few minutes. The moisture that is in the onions is just enough moisture to dissolve the fond that's on the pan, and as the fond is released, it clings to the onions.

Once the onions are browned, add tomato paste. You want to cook a little bit of the sweetness out of the paste; you want it to transform from a bright red to a brick red. It doesn't take very long to do, but it makes a huge difference in the flavor. Once the tomato paste changes color, deglaze the pan with red wine and reduce the wine, getting rid of most of its liquid so that what stays behind is just the flavor of the wine.

While the wine is reducing, add a sachet d'épices containing parsley, a bay leaf, peppercorns, thyme, and a clove of garlic. That will flavor the dish, and later, you can pluck it out as though it were a tea bag. Once the wine is reduced, put the piece of meat back into the pan. Any of the liquids that came from the meat while it was sitting can be added as well.

To switch from dry-heat cooking with fat (sautéing) to moist-heat cooking, introduce veal stock and chicken stock to the pan. The common-sense rule is that the liquid should fill the pan halfway, but in a practical sense, if you don't have enough sauce for every portion of meat, then that amount of liquid is not enough. The amount of liquid will reduce by half, so that might help you judge whether you will have enough sauce. The rule of thumb is to fill the pan a third to half of the way up and bring it to a simmer.

Put the pan into the oven at 350 degrees—with a lid on it so that all of the steam that comes off the liquid is trapped—for about one and a half to two hours. Every 20 or 30 minutes, check on the roast. Each time you check on it, take the pan out, flip the meat top to bottom, and then put it back into the oven.

About two-thirds of the way through the cooking time, introduce some vegetables to the pan, including pearl onions, baby turnips, new potatoes, and baby carrots. Depending on how big or small they are cut, the vegetables may take a longer or shorter amount of time to cook. Because this is a rustic pot roast, you might want to cut the vegetables pretty large.

Selecting the Right Pan for Braising

For braising, you need a pan that is large enough to accommodate what you are cooking, but you don't want it to be too large because the larger it is, the more liquid you will need to add. At some point, you will have to add so much liquid to fill up the pan that it just doesn't make sense, so a snug fit is exactly what you want.

It is important that any pan you use for a braise has a tight-fitting lid because you want to trap the steam that comes off the braise as it cooks. Ideally, the pan that you use should have two handles so that it is easy to take to and from the oven. In addition, a pan with thick walls will temper the heat of the oven very evenly for the meat you are braising.

Once you have determined that the meat is tender and the vegetables are cooked, you can transfer them to a platter. At this point, you can evaluate the quality of the sauce. If it's still a bit watery, heat the pan on the stove, bringing it up to a simmer to cook some of the water out. Taste it for intensity of flavor and level of salt and pepper, but don't season it until it has reduced all the way because if you add salt and then reduce it by half, you're going to end up with something that is twice as salty as you want it to be.

If the texture of the sauce is a little on the light side, you can thicken it with some flour. In a small bowl, add water to some all-purpose flour, stirring it until there are no lumps. This is known as a slurry. If you were to just add flour straight to the sauce, it would cook very quickly and stick to itself, forming lumps.

Cooking Wine

When you come across a recipe that calls for either red or white wine to be used in the cooking, as a general rule, do not waste great wine in a pot. When you're thinking about red wine as a cooking wine, you want a wine that has deep, full color and a tannic structure. Beyond color and tannins, the subtleties of the wine's flavor will probably cook off.

If you have a recipe that calls for red wine, cabernet sauvignon is a great choice. Pinot noir, in contrast, doesn't have a deep, full color, so sauces can look a bit anemic if you use a pinot noir as a cooking wine. For a recipe that calls for white wine, use a wine that has an acidic structure, such as sauvignon blanc. Again, the flavor is less important.

After introducing some of the slurry to the liquid, as soon as the temperature rises to about 180 degrees, the sauce will begin to thicken. Evaluate that thickening before adding more slurry. Pour the sauce off of a ladle and see if it sticks to the back of the ladle, which will tell you that it is thick enough. Whenever you add a raw starch like flour to a liquid mixture, let it cook for about five minutes so that the raw flavor of the flour can work its way out. When the sauce is thick enough to be pulled off of the heat, you can season it with salt and pepper and remove the sachet d'épices.

You can put the meat back into the sauce just to warm it up slightly. Then, bring the meat over to a cutting board. The meat should easily pull away from the bone because the meat is so tender. If you have to struggle with the bones at all, then you haven't cooked the meat enough. Serve the meat in big chunks and let people cut it up themselves.

The sauce of the braise is an integral part of the dish—in fact, it is the dish. In general, don't ever try to serve braised meat without the sauce that it braised in. Furthermore, the sauce is such an integral part of the dish that it should also be served over potatoes or polenta as a side dish.

Lamb Navarin

The biggest difference between stewing and braising is the amount of liquid used and the size of the meat. Stewing has the meat cut up into bite-sized pieces and we'll use a lot of liquid. This meat will be covered with liquid when it's cooking. Braising, we used a much larger piece of meat, multiple portion piece of meat, and we used less liquid.

Start with a piece of lamb shoulder, which is probably one of the few cuts on a lamb that is tough enough to braise or stew. Cut the lamb into big cubes of about one and a half inches on a side. Don't cut the meat too small because as it cooks, it will shrink. In a small bowl, combine salt and pepper—about six times as much salt as pepper—and then add some flour to the mixture. Toss the flour mixture together and let it coat the lamb; this will help the lamb brown a little bit better and add thickness to the sauce.

Turn the heat on the stove all the way up. Add canola oil to a pan and place it on the stove. As you add the cubes of lamb to the pan, be careful not to splash hot fat on yourself. When the meat is brown, take it out of the pan and add the same ingredients as you did for braising—onions and tomato paste—to the pan.

Next, add some garlic to the lamb stew; the sharpness of garlic cuts through any gaminess that might be in the meat. You can also add the same sachet d'épices. Later in the cooking, you can add a nice selection of vegetables to the

stew—including diced turnips, celery, carrots, mushrooms, and potatoes—and you can even use the same slurry that you made for the braise that thickened the cooking liquid.

To deglaze, use red wine, which is important because it brings acidity to the dish, and that acidity will cut through some of the depth of flavor that lamb has—the gaminess.

Selecting the Right Pan for Reducing

If you have to reduce anything quickly, a narrow pan with not very much surface area will take longer than a broad pan with a lot of surface area.

When the lamb has been added back to the pan, add brown stock. However, this time when you add liquid, you won't add it a third to half of the way up the pan. Instead, the lamb needs to be completely covered with liquid. Once the liquid comes up to a boil, reduce it to a simmer and put a tight-fitting lid on top of it.

The boiling drives the fat from the lamb to float on top of the liquid in the pan. Lamb fat has a very pronounced flavor that many people don't like, so you want to skim the fat off the top to avoid a greasy lamb stew.

You can choose to cook the lamb in the oven as you did with the pot roast, but because it's covered in liquid, you don't need heat coming from all sides, so you can actually cook it on top of the stove. However, be careful to keep the heat turned down very low so that the water is at a gentle simmer.

After a few hours, once the lamb and vegetables are fully cooked and the sauce is ready, you can start serving. When serving, remember that the vegetables are just as important to the dish as the meat is, so make sure that the vegetables are well represented on the plate.

This lamb stew is called lamb navarin, and it's typically made in the springtime. If you are making a summer navarin, or summer stew, tomato concassé can be added as a garnish—just before you serve the stew. If flowering thyme is available, when you put it on a hot dish like this, it suddenly becomes very aromatic. Also, a crusty bread is a great side for this dish.

The Browning Process

When browning meat, you can choose how much color you put on it. If you have a big piece of chuck, you might choose to get it very dark. However, lamb is more delicate in flavor, and it's a younger animal, so you might want a little less browning. In fact, if you were sautéing a piece of fish—such as salmon or halibut—you might choose to brown it even slightly less than you would brown lamb. In general, the more full-flavored the meat, the more browning, and the lighter or more delicate the flavor of meat, the less browning.

Evaluating Tenderness

To evaluate tenderness, pierce the meat with a sharp knife. The blade should go in easily, but more importantly, the blade should come out easily. If the knife is sharp, it will go in easily regardless of tenderness, but if the meat is not tender, the knife will be held back by the meat on the way out. Test for tenderness in a few places before deciding that the meat is done.

The same rule applies for determining doneness of vegetables. Take a sharp knife and pierce a vegetable—whether it is a turnip, potato, or carrot—and the knife should go in easily and come out just as easily.

Grilling and Broiling—
Dry-Heat Cooking without Fat
Lesson 9

L ive-fire grilling has been around as long as human beings have been cooking food. Grilling is a dry-heat cooking technique without fat that is in the same family of cooking techniques as broiling, but rather than having heat from above, grilling uses heat from below. Grilling is also a very high-heat cooking technique, and for that reason, you can expect a lot of caramelization, or browning, and with browning comes a lot of flavor—meaty flavors and even roasted flavors.

Grilled Vegetables with Parsley Salad

Shopping List

proportions to taste

zucchini
asparagus
tomatoes
potatoes
other assorted vegetables

Marinade
olive oil
garlic, minced
lemon juice
salt
ground black pepper

Parsley Salad
parsley
garlic
parmesan cheese
olive oil
salt
lemon juice

Before you put vegetables on the grill, lay them out and cut them in big pieces so that you don't have to handle so many different things while they cook. Make a simple marinade to go on all of the vegetables you want to grill that involves olive oil, minced garlic, a squeeze of lemon juice, and salt and pepper.

As a high-moisture vegetable, zucchini will cook very quickly, but you can cut the zucchini in half and score the inside to help it cook even more quickly and more evenly. Asparagus and tomatoes will also cook quickly. All three of these vegetables are naturally tender foods, which is a great quality for a high-heat cooking technique. Potatoes, on the other hand, are a little bit tougher, so if you were to put them onto a grill raw, they would burn on the outside long before they were tender. To make potatoes tender, you can partially cook them ahead of time, boiling them in salted water, letting them cool, and then cutting them in half.

Spoon the marinade over the various vegetables that you want to use. If you are grilling outdoors, be careful about using too much marinade because extra fat can drip off of the vegetables, and when the fat hits the coals below, the fire can flare up.

Turn your grill up to a medium-low heat. There's a lot of sugar in vegetables, and the sugar will brown quickly. Put the vegetables on the grill, placing them so that they cross the bars of the grill, which will give them really nice grill marks. Some people describe this guideline as the ten-and-two guideline, where you begin with your food pointing up to ten o'clock, and later on, if you want crosshatched marks, you turn the food to two o'clock.

When grilling, you want a relaxed sizzle. When working with meat, put your food onto the grill and then let it sit because if you try to move it too quickly, you may discover that it is stuck. With vegetables, this is less of a problem, but you still want to leave them alone while they're cooking.

How Hot Is Your Grill?

To evaluate heat on an outdoor grill that has no knobs to tell you how hot it is, put your hand over the fire—not too close to the flame. If you can only keep your hand there for about three seconds, that is a hot fire. If you can keep your hand over the fire for three to five seconds, that is a medium fire. Finally, if you can keep your hand there for longer than five seconds, that is a low fire. It's important, whether you're grilling inside or outside, that the grill is preheated and clean.

After the vegetables start to get a little color on them from the grill, turn them 90 degrees so that they get some nice crosshatched marks. They should not stick to the grill at this point. Once the vegetables are tender and have some nice markings from the grill on them, they can be taken off the grill.

Once the vegetables come off the grill, they taste great at room temperature, but you might want to season them beyond the marinade. You can make a parsley salad by pulling some parsley into little tufts and adding garlic, parmesan cheese, salt, and olive oil. Because parsley is so full of flavor, you need a powerful vinaigrette, so add plenty of lemon juice. Toss everything together. Then, sprinkle the parsley salad over the grilled vegetables.

Grilled Steak and Lamb Chops

Shopping List

proportions to taste

rib-eye steak
lamb chops
olive oil
salt
ground black pepper
watercress or nasturtiums

Marinade for Lamb Chops
olive oil
rosemary
bay leaf
parsley
garlic
thyme
black peppercorns

***Chimichurri* Sauce for Steak**
shallots
garlic
vinegar
red pepper flakes
salt
olive oil
oregano
parsley
veal stock

A rib-eye steak, or what some people call a cowboy steak, is a really thick steak that comes from the rib of the animal, but the bone has been removed. When grilling steak, it's a good idea to trim the fat off of the steak because as the fat melts and drips down, the fire can flare up. Just so that it doesn't stick to the grill, cover both sides of the cowboy steak with oil and then season it with salt and pepper.

Cut some lamb chops pretty thick, and make a quick marinade using olive oil, rosemary, a bay leaf, parsley, garlic, thyme, and a few peppercorns. Put all of the ingredients into a blender and puree them. Cover the lamb chops with the marinade, which they can sit in for five or six hours in the refrigerator for enhanced flavor.

Turn on the grill, making one end hotter than the other. You want to cook the cowboy steak slowly because it is a thicker, heavier piece of meat, and you want to cook the lamb chops quickly. If you have a charcoal grill, you might want to rake more coals to one side and leave fewer coals on the other side to accomplish this.

Fire on the Grill!

If there is a fire on your grill, simply take the food from where it is on fire, move it to another part of the grill, and let the fire burn out. You also have the option of taking it off the grill entirely.

As soon as you put the steak and lamb chops on the grill, it's important that you evaluate what you see and hear. You should hear a sizzle and see a decent amount of smoke coming off of the grill, which tells you that you are using high heat. If the lamb chop is browning too quickly, you can turn the fire down or move the lamb chop to a cooler part of the grill. A small cut of meat like a lamb chop needs high heat, so it will also get some grill marks pretty quickly. Turn it 90 degrees so that it gets some crosshatching on its first side. Leave the steak alone for a while because it is on the cooler part of the grill. After one side of the pieces of meat has crosshatched grill marks, flip each one and repeat the grilling process for the other side.

The sauce that goes on the cowboy steak is a sauce that is often used in Brazil called *chimichurri*, which is an herb-based sauce. To make *chimichurri*, mince some shallots and put them into a bowl with some garlic. Think of *chimichurri* as a vinaigrette, so add vinegar and then season it with some pepper flakes

and plenty of salt. Then, stir olive oil into the mixture. Use about 50 percent vinegar and 50 percent olive oil, which is a little more powerful than a regular vinaigrette. Finally, add herbs, such as fresh oregano and chopped parsley.

Determining Doneness

The safest way to determine doneness with a thick steak is to use a digital meat thermometer, inserting it into the thickest part of the meat. Pull the steak off the grill when the thermometer reaches about 130 to 135 degrees for a medium-rare steak and when it reaches about 128 to 130 degrees for a rare steak.

To add some meatiness to this sauce, you can add veal stock that has been reduced to a glace. When you add it, make sure that it gets dispersed throughout. Adding hot meat glace to the mixture will bring out the flavor of the herbs, garlic, and shallots.

When the cowboy steak is fully grilled, move it to a plate and add peppery greens, such as watercress or nasturtiums, which is a classic garnish for grilled beef. Finally, spoon some *chimichurri* sauce over the steak and serve it with some grilled potatoes. When the lamb chops are fully grilled, serve them with some grilled vegetables and parsley salad.

If you wanted to broil the cowboy steak and lamb chops instead of grilling them, you could do it in your oven by setting it on broil. The difference would be that the meats would cook from the top down rather than from the bottom up.

Grilled Mahi Mahi with Pineapple Salsa

Shopping List

proportions to taste

mahi mahi
vegetable oil
salt

Pineapple Salsa
red onion, minced
jicama, julienned
red pepper, diced
spicy chiles or jalapeños, minced
serrano pepper
pineapple, diced
lime juice
salt
cilantro, roughly chopped
vegetable oil

Mahi mahi is a great fish to grill because it is a firm fish that doesn't flake quite as easily as some other fish. If you're grilling outside, it's imperative that your grill is hot before you put the fish on it. In addition, blot the fish dry before you put it on the grill because it will stick to the grill if it is wet. Furthermore, oil the bars of the grill just prior to putting the fish on the grill; if you oil the bars and then wait to add the fish, though, the oil will be sticky by the time you add the fish. Rub a little bit of oil on each side of the fish as well and season it with salt, which acts as a barrier to the fish sticking to the grill.

Place the fish on the grill with its presentation side down first. In other words, find the side of the fish that looks the most attractive and that should be the side that goes onto the grill first. That way, when you present the fish on a plate, the fish will look its best.

Start grilling the fish on a fairly hot grill, and then, if it's cooking quickly and you feel like you need to move it to a cooler spot, you can. On a hot grill, the protein hits the grill and immediately seizes up, and as it seizes, it pulls away from the bars and frees itself. Therefore, don't fuss with the fish too quickly; it needs a chance to sear so that it can free itself from the bars. In addition, you might want to avoid the process of making crosshatched marks when you're grilling fish because the more you manipulate fish, the more likely it is to stick to the grill.

Regulating the Heat of Your Grill

To regulate a gas grill, simply turn the knob that regulates heat up or down, but if you are dealing with charcoal, sometimes fanning the flames, blowing off some of the ash, or even stirring the coals so that the ash falls off will bring new life to the fire.

You can monitor the progress of the fish by seeing it turn opaque. As it cooks, it turns opaque from the bottom toward the top. You want to make sure that it cooks to the center.

Pineapple salsa goes well with grilled mahi mahi. The ingredients include red onions, jicama, red pepper, spicy chiles, serrano, and plenty of pineapple. To these ingredients, add some lime juice and a little bit of salt. Then, add some chopped cilantro. To finish the salsa, add some vegetable oil and stir everything together.

Make sure that you add enough lime juice so that it's bright with acidity because as the salsa sits, some of the moisture will come out of the vegetables, which will water down the dressing that is on the salsa. Therefore, the salsa should be assertive with acidity when you begin. Think of the salsa more as a colorful salad.

When the mahi mahi is grilled, put just a little bit of the salsa on the bottom of a plate and then lay the fish on top of the salsa. Then, put some salsa on top of the fish as well.

Grilled Nectarine with Ice Cream

Shopping List

proportions to taste

nectarines
butter
honey
fruit sauce
caramel ice cream

To go along with the grilled mahi mahi dish, make a very simple dessert: a grilled nectarine served with ice cream. The beauty of a grilled piece of fruit as dessert is that especially when you're outside and the fire of the grill is dying down, you can use that gentle heat to grill something with a lot of sugar, such as a peach or nectarine.

Before putting the nectarine on the grill, melt a small amount of butter and add to it the same amount of honey. Then, cut the nectarine in half and roll it in that mixture. Put it over the dying embers of the fire, and that gentle heat will soften and caramelize it.

On a plate, drizzle a very simple fruit sauce and then lay the grilled nectarine on top of the sauce. Finally, add a scoop of caramel-flavored ice cream to the plate—along with possibly your favorite cookie or a little bit of cake.

Stocks and Broths—The Foundation

Lesson 10

Stocks and broths are some of the most basic preparations you will find in kitchens anywhere in the world. They draw their flavor from bones, meats, and vegetables. They are easy to make and easy to store, and they are supremely versatile. You can use them for everything from making soups and sauces to cooking grains and vegetables. In addition to helping you master the technique, this lesson will help you understand how stocks are categorized based on the ingredients that give them flavor and on their method of preparation.

White Chicken Stock

Shopping List

proportions to taste

chicken bones, cleaned and rinsed
cold water
mirepoix (onions, carrots, and celery)

sachet d'épices (parsley, a bay leaf, peppercorns, thyme, and a clove of garlic)

A white chicken stock is a stock in which the bones, meat, and vegetables are not browned at all. Start to finish, this stock will take about four hours to cook.

To make chicken stock, start with some chicken bones that have been rinsed. You might have the chicken's carcass with a little bit of attached meat, some wings, some leg bones, and maybe even a chicken foot. The wings and the feet have a lot of gelatin, so they'll give you a much richer stock in a way that commercial stocks don't have body.

The First Restaurant

In the early 1600s, there were no restaurants as we know them today. The very first restaurant that came along in the late 1600s was a restaurant that served only one thing: a restorative broth. The word "restaurant" comes from the restorative broth that was served in that very first restaurant.

Take the bones and put them into a pot that has cold water in it. It's good to start with cold water because the goal is to draw the flavor out of the bones—not to seal the flavor inside. Then, turn on the heat. As the water begins to simmer, all the protein that is water-soluble will begin to coagulate with the heat, and it will float up to the top. By skimming the protein and excess fat off the top of the water every 30 minutes or so, you will end up with a stock that is much clearer than it would be otherwise.

Stocks and Broth— What's the Difference?

Some people make a distinction between broth and stock. A broth is cooked with more meat and, therefore, has more of a meaty flavor. The bones are what give your stock gelatin and body, and the meat is what gives your stock a meaty flavor.

In the last two hours of cooking, add some cut vegetables—what is called a mirepoix—to your stock. For example, add about 50 percent onions, 25 percent carrots, and 25 percent celery. A ratio for a stock is about eight pounds of bones per pound of mirepoix, which results in about a gallon of stock.

Another thing that will add a bit of flavor is what the French call a sachet d'épices, or a little bag of spices. To make one, gather parsley, a bay leaf, peppercorns, thyme, and a clove of garlic into what is basically a tea bag. However, because you are going to be straining this stock, you can just add those spices directly to the stock.

After about four hours, if you manipulate the bones, they should be just at the point where they will fall apart easily—joint upon joint. The meat should all be tender, and the bones should come apart very easily.

If the bones are not falling apart, then you probably haven't drawn as much flavor out of them as you could. If they fell apart two hours into cooking and you continued to cook for two more hours, then the flavors would start to get dark and deep and a little bit muddy.

After your stock has been cooking for about two hours, periodically taste it to see what you think about the flavor. Is it still watery? Does it have body? Does it have a full chicken flavor? Is the flavor starting to get a little tired and muddy? Do this once or twice while you make a chicken stock, and very quickly you will start to recognize what a good stock is and when it should come off the heat.

Once your stock is ready to be strained, strain it through a colander. Pour it away from yourself so that you don't burn yourself by splashing hot liquid on you. If you want to strain your stock through something finer, it will take some of the little bits and pieces of chicken meat or the herbs out. Once you've strained the liquid off of the bones, they can be discarded.

Your chicken stock is now ready to be used. You could also chill it and keep it in the refrigerator for about a week, or you could freeze it and keep it for about three months.

Brown Veal Stock

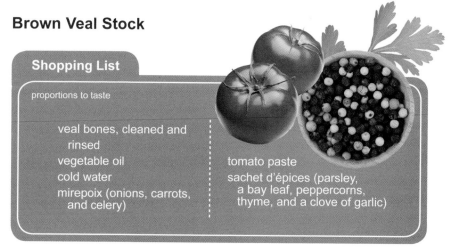

Shopping List

proportions to taste

veal bones, cleaned and rinsed
vegetable oil
cold water
mirepoix (onions, carrots, and celery)

tomato paste
sachet d'épices (parsley, a bay leaf, peppercorns, thyme, and a clove of garlic)

A brown veal stock is a stock in which the meat and vegetables are browned before you cook them in liquid. To make veal stock, start with veal bones, such as veal neck bones. No matter how good a butcher you are, there will always be a little bit of meat left on the bones. As a young animal, veal has a lot of gelatin.

You can find veal bones in a butcher shop, or if you go to the meat counter in a supermarket, you can probably find some sort of bones. Ask the person behind the counter.

To begin making your stock, you need to roast the veal bones. Add a little bit of oil in the bottom of a roasting pan, and then just dump the bones in. Put the pan in the oven at about 400 degrees for about 45 minutes to an hour.

When the veal bones are ready to be taken out of the oven, you will see that they will be nicely browned. If they are done, gather the bones and place them into a pot of cold water.

On the bottom of the roasting pan, there is a little bit of fond, which you want to try and capture. Add a little bit of water to deglaze the pan. You can even turn the heat on. You will notice that the color of the fond will start to color the water, and that is really where your stock begins. Something with a flat end on it is great for scraping up the bottom. It will only take you a few minutes, but it's well worth the effort.

A veal stock cooks for six to eight hours, depending on how big the bones are cut. After about six hours, the liquid is reduced, and you can add vegetables—a mirepoix—and tomato paste. You will have to brown the vegetables and tomato paste before adding them to the stock. Start by browning the onions in hot fat, and then add the carrots and celery. At the very end, add the tomato paste, which should cook so that it goes from a bright red to sort of a brick red, giving it a much deeper, fuller flavor.

Stock Pots

Traditionally, stock pots are fairly narrow pots that are deep. With a narrow pot, you get less evaporation, and with a taller pot, it takes up less real estate on the stove.

After adding the vegetables and tomato paste, you can add a sachet d'épices, which has in it parsley, a bay leaf, peppercorns, thyme, and a clove of garlic. After two additional hours of cooking, the flavor will come out of the vegetables and herbs.

Your completed veal stock will look a little different from your chicken stock. For example, the veal bones won't fall apart quite so readily. However, you should still periodically taste your veal stock just as you tasted your chicken stock. You're looking for a full, meaty flavor. You're also looking for body and for the flavor of the vegetables and herbs. When you start to taste the flavors getting a little muddy, pull it off the heat.

Then, strain your stock. If you strain it through a fine mesh cheesecloth, one of the challenges that you might face in the beginning is that it may get clogged with some of the particulate, so try to help the liquid get through.

Your brown stock will keep very well if you chill it down and refrigerate it. It can be in the refrigerator for as long as a week, or you can freeze it.

A glace is stock that is cooked down until most of its moisture has been removed. Think of it almost like a commercial base, which you can add water to in order to make a stock. In this case, your glace would be called *glace de viande*, or veal glace.

Try to cool your stock down quickly. Put it into a larger bowl of ice water, which will take the heat out of it very quickly. The faster you can get it in the refrigerator, the longer it will last.

Fish Stock

The flavors of fish are easily destroyed, so don't cook your fish stock—or fish fume—too long or too hard. The fish bones that you use can come from any sort of white fish that doesn't have a lot of fat, such as cod, sole, flounder, or halibut. However, fish like salmon, mackerel, and sardines are not good choices.

To start, the fish bones have to be cleaned pretty well and rinsed. Make sure to remove any blood, guts, or gills, and take the head off. After the bones have been cleaned, cut them into small pieces.

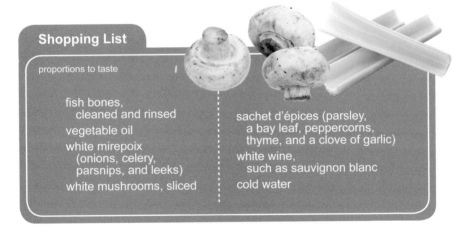

Shopping List

proportions to taste

fish bones,
    cleaned and rinsed
vegetable oil
white mirepoix
    (onions, celery,
    parsnips, and leeks)
white mushrooms, sliced

sachet d'épices (parsley,
    a bay leaf, peppercorns,
    thyme, and a clove of garlic)
white wine,
    such as sauvignon blanc
cold water

Then, take the bones and sweat them—which means cook them without coloring them—in a pot that has a little bit of oil in the bottom. Fish bones are so delicate that as they cook, they will begin to fall apart almost immediately (after a few minutes). Be careful not to color the bones because you want your stock to be

a nice light color. As the fish bones start to fall apart, first the meat falls off the bones and then the bones themselves begin to collapse and mat down.

Next, add a mirepoix to your stock—just the way you did with each of the other stocks. However, this time, use a white mirepoix because you want to keep your stock light in color. Therefore, replace the carrots with parsnips and leeks and then add those vegetables plus sliced white mushrooms to the stock. Finally, add a sachet d'épices. Be careful that it doesn't stick to the bottom of the pot and begin to brown.

The liquids that go into a fish stock are water and wine. For example, a sauvignon blanc has a nice hit of acidity, which is important to balance what otherwise might come across as a bit of a fishy taste. Use about one-fifth wine and four-fifths water.

You want the bones to just barely be covered with liquid. The more water you add, the longer you're going to have to cook it later in the process to reduce it in order to get the flavor you want. In addition, the more you have to cook it and reduce it, the longer the fish bones cook, and the fish flavor starts to get muddy very quickly.

Bring the contents of the pot up to a simmer, and then skim the liquid very well. After about 45 minutes to an hour, the bones will come completely apart, and the vegetables will give up their flavor. It will smell nice and fresh. Then, strain the stock, and taste it.

With this stock especially, you need to chill it immediately in the refrigerator because fish spoils very quickly.

Chicken Noodle Soup

Stock Tips

Stocks don't have to be all about meat and fish. You could also make a vegetable stock by starting with a basic mirepoix and adding mushrooms and some fennel, for example. When making a stock—whether you are using chicken, veal, fish, shellfish, or vegetables—you want to use good-quality ingredients. Likewise, pay attention to your technique. Don't boil your stock really hard; otherwise, the fat may emulsify, which would not lead to a clear stock.

You can make a very simple chicken soup from the white chicken stock that you made earlier. First, taste the stock. You want to make sure that it has enough flavor; you could always reduce it to concentrate the flavor.

Season the stock with a little bit of salt and pepper and then add a selection of vegetables, such as mushrooms and mirepoix. Next, add some chicken meat that has been shredded and some noodles that have been cooked.

Finally, add some herbs, such as parsley, tarragon, and thyme. Make sure to remove any stems from the herbs before adding them because they are woody and wouldn't taste very good. Strip off just the more tender leaves, and then chop them.

Let your soup simmer for 5 or 10 minutes. Be careful that you don't cook it too long because the pasta will fall apart if you do. Check the seasoning one last time, and don't be shy about adding salt. Your soup is done.

The Stir-Fry Dance—
Dry-Heat Cooking with Fat

S tir-frying is nothing more than sautéing with a Chinese passport; it involves dry-heat cooking with fat. Everything you have already learned about sautéing can be brought to bear on stir-frying in this lesson. French chef Fernand Point said that success in the kitchen is really the result of a lot of small things properly done, and that's the mindset that you need to have when you stir-fry. The process of stir-frying unfolds quickly, but if you pay attention to the details and focus on your technique, you will create a wonderful stir-fry dish.

Vietnamese Noodle Salad

Shopping List

proportions to taste

vermicelli noodles, cooked
lettuce, finely shredded
cabbage, finely shredded
bean sprouts
mint leaves, cut

Cilantro-Lime Sauce
Thai bird chiles, minced
garlic, minced
ginger, minced
lime juice
sugar
soy sauce
water
cilantro, chopped
peanuts, chopped

Vegetable Stir-Fry
canola oil
onions, finely chopped
carrots, finely chopped
red peppers, finely chopped
shitake mushrooms,
  finely chopped
soy sauce
broccoli, precooked
scallion oil

This is a Vietnamese dish that is basically a noodle salad that has stir-fry vegetables on top of it. It is a vegetarian dish. Start by adding finely shredded lettuce and cabbage, bean sprouts, and mint leaves torn into small pieces to cooked rice noodles. Then, set this salad aside.

Because you want to be ready to serve your warm stir-fry directly on top of the noodle salad, you can transfer the salad onto a platter. However, once the noodles are cooked, they have a tendency of sticking to themselves. To avoid this, moisten them with a little bit of water, and they'll come apart. You want to make a little nest with the salad so that the stir-fry can sit right in the middle of it. You can make the salad ahead of time; it can sit out for about a few hours.

Using a mortar and pestle, pound Thai bird chiles, garlic, and ginger into an aromatic paste. If you don't have a mortar and pestle, you don't have to pound the ingredients; instead, they can be sliced very finely or minced using a knife. The chiles can be very hot, so exercise caution when adding them to your sauce. If you don't like your food too hot, then start with half the quantity and move up to the full quantity.

Regulating Heat with Stir-Fry

Professional chefs in Asia have stoves that are incredibly powerful. They deliver a tremendous amount of heat to this pan, so unless you cut the food very small, it will probably burn on the outside before it is cooked on the inside. The stoves in the United States don't get nearly as hot, but American chefs still cook the food the same way. When stir-frying, they regulate the heat in a similar manner as when sautéing, but they are most likely going to keep the heat at its highest point for the entire time.

Moisten the paste with lime juice. To cut the acidity of the lime juice, add sugar. Add soy sauce on the top, along with a few tablespoons of water to make the soy sauce less bold. Garnish with chopped cilantro, and set next to the platter that holds the salad. Chop some peanuts and set them aside as well.

When stir-frying, use a wok, sauté pan, or cast-iron pan. The steeply sloped sides of a wok are designed to deliver the food back to the hottest part of the pan repeatedly. Traditionally, woks are made of very thin steel, but you can find woks

that are a bit heavier. In fact, a cast-iron wok holds heat really well. If you don't have a wok, you can use a sauté pan or a nicely seasoned cast-iron pan.

To prepare for stir-frying, line up the noodle salad, the sauce, the chopped peanuts, assorted vegetables—such as onions, carrots, red peppers, and shitake mushrooms—soy sauce, scallion oil, and canola oil. To prepare the scallion oil, cook some scallion in a little bit of oil and puree it in a blender. In addition, precook broccoli in a pot of boiling water (seasoned with salt) for about 40 seconds as soon as you start stir-frying.

To begin, add canola oil, or any oil that can withstand high temperatures, to a very hot wok or heavy skillet. When you add the oil into your wok, it should start to smoke almost immediately. Quickly stir-fry the onions first so that some of the harsh, sulfuric compounds of the onion can start to vaporize. Then, add carrots, red peppers, and shitake mushrooms—all finely chopped.

Spread the vegetables to the edges of the wok and pour a small amount of soy sauce into the base. Allow the soy sauce to reduce, and then toss it with the vegetables, adding the precooked broccoli. Turn off the heat and adjust the seasoning of the vegetables, adding salt or soy sauce if necessary after tasting.

Spoon the warm vegetables on top of the noodle salad. Dress the salad with a bit of scallion oil, which will become really aromatic as it hits the hot vegetables. Spoon the cilantro-lime dipping sauce over the salad, and garnish with the chopped peanuts. Serve the dish with extra dipping sauce at the table.

How Hot Is Your Wok?

If you want to evaluate how hot your wok is, sprinkle a little bit of water into the wok and watch to see if it skitters around—almost as if it is riding on a cushion of steam—and then evaporates very quickly. It actually should not evaporate as quickly as you may think because the steam between the droplet and the wok insulates the water from the heat below.

Shaking Beef

A Vietnamese dish called shaking beef was named by Vietnamese chefs who saw French chefs put meat into a pan and shake it around. They were used to doing something very different with a wok.

Ma Po Tofu

This is a spicy and savory dish that was named after the grandmother who used to make it. It comes from the Szechuan region of China. This is a vegetarian dish—except for the oyster sauce, for which you can find substitutions.

Start by laying out all of the ingredients that you will need. Onions, garlic, and ginger often serve as the beginning of many different stir-fry dishes because when you add them to a hot wok, they explode with fragrance. That is also why they are considered to be aromatic vegetables.

Shopping List

proportions to taste

onions, thinly sliced	red peppers
garlic, minced	bean sprouts
ginger, minced	firm tofu, diced and fried
fermented black bean paste	white pepper, cayenne pepper, or chili pepper
oyster sauce	cilantro, chopped
Korean chili paste	Szechuan peppercorns, ground
water	vegetable oil
dried shitake mushrooms	sesame oil
snow peas or romano beans	cilantro, minced
	rice, cooked

You also need to have some sauce condiments ready. Fermented black bean paste—which is not made with black beans, but with soy beans that turn black when you ferment them—has a wonderful savory flavor that will flavor a large amount of vegetables, tofu, and even rice. Oyster sauce is savory as well; it's made from the liquid that comes from oysters, which then is allowed to reduce to become very concentrated. Korean chili paste has a good deal of heat to it, but it also has a wonderful richness of depth that is captivating.

Dried shitake mushrooms will lend a meatiness to this dish—which is especially helpful because tofu doesn't have a tremendous amount of flavor on its own. Soak the shitake mushrooms in water until they are tender. Then, remove the stem, which tends to be really woody, and cut the mushrooms into thin slivers.

Wok Hey: "The Breath of the Wok"

The idea behind the expression *wok hey* is that food cooked quickly and assertively in a wok seems to almost "forget" that it has been cooked. It retains its original freshness and vitality. In preparing a stir-fry dish, you want your guests to taste the breath of the wok.

The vegetables that go into this dish are beans (snow peas or romano beans, for example), red peppers, and bean sprouts. The tofu should be firm tofu, which should be diced up ahead of time. Then, you should fry the tofu in hot fat until it becomes golden on the outside and develops a little bit of a skin, which takes about three to four minutes at about 350 degrees. Frying it will give it more flavor, but it will also help it hold its shape in the stir-fry.

Then, you want to make sure that you have some finishing spices to add at the very end of cooking this dish. If you want your stir-fry to be on the hotter end of the spectrum, use white pepper (which is traditionally used in China and has an interesting sour flavor), cayenne pepper, or chili pepper. You can also sprinkle some chopped cilantro on the top of the dish. If you add cilantro any earlier than the end, the aroma will be lost. You can also add Szechuan

peppercorns, which are not true peppercorns. Instead, they have a little bit of a numbing quality, but in a stir-fry—when they are surrounded by a lot of vegetable matter—Szechuan peppercorns give an intriguing textural and flavor quality that is very appealing.

Before stir-frying, make sure that your wok is nice and hot. Test how hot your wok is by using a little splash of water and watching to see if it sizzles. Then, dump the water out. Once the wok is hot enough, start by adding some oil and then the aromatic vegetables. After the aromatic vegetables explode into flavor, add any other vegetables. The vegetables will bring some of the heat of the oil down, so make sure that your wok is on high heat. Then, add the shitake mushrooms. If you notice that your vegetables are beginning to scorch, it just means that you have to keep them moving a little faster.

Mix the sauce ingredients—black bean paste, oyster sauce, and chili paste—in a small bowl with a little water. You don't want to add too much water because if you do, you'll end up simmering the vegetables; you just want enough water to keep the heat very high. At this point, you can also add the tofu to the wok, just to warm it up.

Seasoning Rice

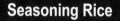

Chefs who cook rice in America typically season the water that they cook the rice in with a little bit of salt, but in China, the rice is typically cooked without any seasoning. The idea is that the stir-fry will have plenty of seasoning to flavor the rice.

After you are done cooking the ingredients in the wok, add your finishing spices. After turning the wok off, at the very end, add sesame oil (an aromatic oil) and cilantro. Your stir-fry is now done; you can taste it and add salt if needed. You can also add a splash of water if the sauce seems to be a little tight. Start to finish, the stir-frying probably takes no more than three to five minutes. Finally, spoon your stir-fry on top of some precooked rice.

How to Cook Rice

To cook rice, first measure the rice, pour it into a bowl or colander, and wash it well to eliminate the surface starch. When washing the rice, you will notice that the starch on the surface of the rice will begin to cloud the water very quickly. After rinsing, discard the starch. This step ensures that the cooked rice won't be sticky. If your rice is a little sticky, it makes it easy to use chopsticks, but if it is too sticky, it becomes objectionable.

For every type of rice that you cook, there will be a measured amount of water that is appropriate for that rice. For example, cook brown rice in two and a half times as much water as rice. For converted rice, use two times as much water as rice.

Bring the water to a boil, add the rice, return to a boil, and then turn down the heat to a simmer. You don't want it to boil hard because you don't want the rice to break up. Once it is at a simmer, cover the rice and let it cook for about 15 minutes.

The rice is done when there is no more free liquid in the pan and when the grains are tender all the way through. If you're curious as to whether it's fully cooked, taste it; there should be no chalky core at the center of the rice.

Allow the rice to sit for about 10 minutes after it has cooked, and then fluff it with a fork to break up any stickiness. The rice will stay warm for probably an hour or more, so you can just set it aside while cooking the ma po tofu.

Herbs and Spices—
Flavor on Demand
Lesson 12

Herbs and spices have been used by human beings for as long as vegetation has been consumed by human beings. For thousands of years, we have added herbs and spices to our food as flavoring, but we have also put them to work as preservatives, preventive tonics, and even medicines. Plants have evolved to produce a series of phytochemicals that have distinctive aromas and flavors—many of which are protective—and we have learned to leverage that knowledge to make the food that we eat safer.

Salt

Kosher salt is a very pure salt. Because it is ground coarsely, nothing needs to be added to it to make it flow freely or keep it from caking up. Iodized salt, on the other hand, is ground a little bit more finely than kosher salt. Iodine is added to salt to keep it from caking up or to keep it flowing freely. There is also a flavor that is associated with iodine, so iodized salt is not as true a flavor as kosher salt.

Sel gris, or gray salt, is simply seawater that has been dehydrated until all of the water is gone and everything that was inherent in the seawater is still in the salt. *Sel gris* has more complexity and more minerals than other salts. There may even be some plant or animal life that makes its way into the salt, so there are health concerns, but the flavor is compelling and complex.

Maldon salt is an unrefined salt. As it crystallizes, it takes on a very delicate, flaked conformation so that when you put it on food and it crunches on your tongue, it breaks apart very easily. It dries in sort of a conical pyramid formation.

Ground Salt

The finer salt is ground, the more aggressive it will seem on your palate. A finely ground salt, for example, may be used on top of popcorn. Coarsely ground salt, on the other hand, is less aggressive on the palate.

Pepper

Black pepper, green pepper, and white pepper all come from the same plant and all start as a green peppercorn. To turn a green peppercorn into black pepper, the peppercorn is soaked very briefly and then dried. Enzymatic browning takes hold, and its color changes from green to brown. As it dries, the outside of the peppercorn shrinks. Instead, if you soaked and fermented a green peppercorn for about a week, you could then grind the outside off to create white peppercorns.

Some people like the flavor of the green peppercorns because it is vegetal. Others like black pepper because it has a fuller, richer, almost roasted flavor. Still others believe that white peppercorn is appropriate for white preparations, such as a béchamel sauce or mashed potatoes, where you don't want to see flecks of black in your food.

Tasting Pepper

If you close your eyes and taste these three peppers, you will notice that they taste very different. Green pepper tastes vegetal; it has the burn of pepper but tastes very green. Black pepper has a full, rich, satisfying flavor. White pepper tastes a little bit sour.

Szechuan peppercorn is not a true peppercorn. It has a numbing effect on your palate—specifically on your cheeks and tongue. Its numbing quality can be downplayed by toasting it in a pan before you grind it up and use it.

Salt and Pepper Combined

The combination of salt and pepper is one of the most pervasive flavorings, embraced by almost every culture in the world. One of the reasons that we add salt to our food is that it has very powerful antimicrobial properties. In addition to adding flavor, pepper is protective against botulism, but it also makes bacteria more susceptible to the plant chemicals that are found in herbs and spices.

Herbs

Both herbs and spices come from plants, but herbs tend to be the tender, leafy parts of the plant whereas spices are seeds, roots, stems, and tougher parts of the plant. Therefore, sometimes the difference between herbs and spices is muddied.

Herbs can be classified into resinous herbs and tender herbs, or fine herbs. Resinous herbs tend to dry very well because of the oils and resin in them while fine herbs don't dry nearly as well. For example, parsley is a fine herb, and while you can find it in the store dried, it doesn't have much flavor and its color is not nearly as vibrant as it is when it's fresh. The good news is that fresh parsley is readily available.

On the other hand, resinous herbs—such as rosemary, thyme, and bay leaves—dry marvelously well. In fact, some people actually prefer the dried herb to the fresh herb in these cases because the dried herb tends to be less aggressive. For example, when it's fresh, rosemary can be very powerful in resinous and piney qualities; in contrast, while it's still strong, the dried herb is not nearly as aggressive.

Dried versus Fresh Herbs

Surprisingly, you should use less of a dried herb than you would if the same herb were fresh. This may seem counterintuitive because you might think that you need less of a fresh herb—which is more vital and stronger than a dried herb—but there's actually more water in fresh herbs, and water doesn't really have flavor. Therefore, a half to a third of a dried herb translates into two or three times as much of a fresh herb.

Aromatic herbs, such as mint and sage, seem to dry pretty well because of their strong aroma. For that reason, dried sage is an herb that is handy to have on hand. In addition, dried mint makes a delicious mint tea, and the aroma of the tea is every bit as powerful as it would be if it were fresh.

Whether you use dried or fresh herbs, recognize that herbs are perishable. It's easy to tell when a fresh herb is getting old because it starts to wilt or decay a little bit, but it's less easy to tell when a dried herb is getting old. However, if a dried herb no longer smells like the herb that it is, it's time to replace it. As long as you keep your herbs sealed in a jar, they can live in your cupboard for about a year. After that, you might think about replacing them.

Spices

It is best to buy spices whole and then grind them as you need them because they are perishable—just as herbs are. When your spices no longer smell like what they are, then it's time to get rid of them. If you buy spices whole, have a spice grinder or small coffee grinder that you reserve just for the purpose of grinding spices because if you use it for coffee and for spices, your coffee might taste like curry or your curry might taste like coffee.

Salt: Spice or Mineral?

Salt is often incorrectly categorized as a spice, but it is a mineral. Salt comes from seawater. Some salt can be trapped underground, and as it dehydrates, it crystallizes. Then, it can be mined from underground.

When you have whole spices, you can toast them to round out the flavor, making them much richer and less aggressive. To toast cumin seeds, for example, place them into a hot pan and turn the heat up high, swirling the seeds in the pan. Initially, you won't see much happening, but as the heat hits those herbs, you'll start to get the aroma of those herbs coming out of the pan. The longer the herbs are on the heat and the hotter the pan is, the more you have to concern yourself with keeping them moving.

Once you have smelled the aroma of the seeds, you should watch for the color of the spice to darken slightly. To more easily see the color change, you can compare some untoasted seeds with those that you are toasting. Then, you might see a few wisps of smoke coming off the pan. When you see smoke, keep the herbs moving. Toward the end of the toasting process, you may see a few seeds popping—depending on what the seed is. By the time you see the smoke, it's important to keep the seeds moving almost constantly. Finally, take them out of the hot pan so that they can cool and not burn from the heat of the pan.

Mint and Cilantro Chutney

Shopping List

proportions to taste

cilantro
serrano chiles
green onion, cut
mint
lime juice
salt
sugar

Cheese with Popped Spices
cheese, such as fromage blanc
mustard seeds
cumin seeds
nigella seeds
canola oil
crispy bread or pita chips

To make a fresh herb chutney from India, start by breaking some cilantro in half and then dropping it into a blender. Then, add some serrano chiles. If you have one large chili, don't use the entire thing because it could make the chutney too spicy. Cut a green onion into chunks and then add it to the blender. Finally, you want the chutney to be aromatic, so add some mint leaves.

To get the blender to spin, you might have to add some liquid, so squeeze some lime juice into the blender. You don't want too much moisture in the mixture, but a little bit will help the herbs catch in the blender and start to liquefy themselves. If the herbs don't catch right away, turn the blender off, pressing the mixture down to the blades, and then turn it back on. Blend the herbs until they are pureed, and then taste and season them with salt and—to bring out the sweetness of the herbs—a little bit of sugar as well.

This aromatic green chutney can be used to accompany a dish of fresh cheese, such as fromage blanc, with popped spices. Start with some fresh herbs, including a few different colors of mustard seeds, cumin seeds, and nigella seeds—which are black seeds that lend a savory oniony flavor.

In a hot pan, introduce some cooking oil, such as canola oil. Then, add the seeds and swirl them in the oil. Initially, they are going to cook; then, they will start to pop. Once they start to pop, put a lid over the pan and continue to cook and swirl the seeds for about 15 to 20 seconds. Keep them moving so that they don't burn. The spices will have a much deeper, fuller flavor after being popped.

Use the spices and the oil that they cooked in to flavor the cheese. Put the cheese onto a plate, breaking it up so that it is a little bit craggy. Therefore, there should be plenty of places for the spices to collect. Then, place some of the chutney around the outside of the cheese, add some crispy bread or pita chips, and pour the spices and oil on top of the dish. The spices serve as not just a flavoring, but also as a textural element; they are crunchy, and they make this a satisfying dish.

Roasted Tomato and Saffron Vinaigrette

Shopping List

proportions to taste

mustard	orange zest
shallots, minced	red pepper flakes
garlic, minced	saffron
red wine vinegar	tomatoes, chopped and roasted
capers	mild French olive oil
thyme, chopped	salt
orange juice	pastis

This vinaigrette utilizes one of the most expensive herbs you will ever buy—saffron, which is the stamen from a very tiny crocus. It is expensive because each blossom only has three or four threads of saffron, and they have to be harvested by hand. The male portion of the crocus is a little yellow thread while the female portion, which is more desirable, is a red thread. If you see saffron with too many yellow threads in it, that's indicative of poor quality. If you buy saffron that has been ground to a powder, it might have a lot of the male thread in it, so it is best to buy saffron in threads.

You want to protect both the aroma and the color of saffron by keeping it dry and shielding it from light. To do this, keep it in a tin can in your pantry, and inside the can, enclose it in a small plastic bag. It usually keeps very nicely for a year or more. To draw the color and aroma out of saffron, soak it in warm water.

To make the vinaigrette, start by building the flavors of bouillabaisse, which is a tomato and saffron seafood stew, into a vinaigrette. To a bowl, add mustard—which is an emulsifier—shallots, and garlic. Then, add some vinegar just to bring out the flavors of those elements. Add some capers, chopped thyme, orange zest, and pepper flakes. Finally, add some threads of saffron.

Chop up some tomatoes and roast them under the broiler of your oven or on the grill. They should blacken on the outside, but more importantly, the flesh of the tomato should completely collapse. Once they are cooked, you'll see how

easily the skin will peel away. Then, chop up the pulp, seeds, and liquid and introduce that to your vinaigrette.

Next, add a mild French olive oil, stirring it in with a whisk so that the mixture stays as a loose emulsion. Use about three times as much oil as vinegar. Because there is so much moisture in the tomatoes, the mixture will emulsify fairly easily. If the emulsion separates, just stir it or shake it, and it will come back together again.

Season the vinaigrette with salt and add just a little bit of orange juice because it complements saffron well. Then, the secret ingredient is pastis, which is an anise-flavored liqueur that sometimes makes its way into a bouillabaisse. If your vinaigrette tastes good off the spoon, then it is probably not assertive enough. If that is the case, add more salt and pastis to taste. This vinaigrette is great to have on hand. It goes well with grilled fish, grilled meats, and grilled vegetables.

Dukkah

Shopping List

proportions to taste

sesame seeds, toasted
cumin, toasted
coriander, toasted
hazelnuts, toasted
salt
ground black pepper

To make dukkah, which is a spice mix from the Eastern Mediterranean, start with some toasted sesame seeds, toasted cumin, toasted coriander, and toasted hazelnuts. Combine them into a spice grinder and grind them into a fine powder.

You need to be careful when you are grinding nuts because if you grind them for too long, you will be left with nut butter, which is not what you want. Once you have ground the mixture, stir in some salt and black pepper. Dukkah keeps pretty well for about a month in a plastic bag, which protects it from air and moisture.

Traditionally, dukkah is spooned into a dish and served alongside a small dish of a very flavorful olive oil with some bread for dipping. In the Eastern Mediterranean, people will often dip the bread first into the olive oil and then into the dukkah, which cuts through the aggressive nature of the oil and flavors the bread.

Spice Rub for Pork

Shopping List

proportions to taste

thyme, ground
coriander
red pepper flakes
curry powder
paprika
cumin
pork tenderloin, diced

parsley
garlic
lemon juice
olive oil
red grapes
salt

To make this spice rub—which is inspired by the Moorish occupation of Spain, so the spices are exotic—start with ground thyme, coriander, pepper flakes, curry powder, paprika, and cumin. Add that mixture to some pork tenderloin that has been diced up. Then, introduce some parsley, garlic, lemon juice, and olive oil to the pork as well. Stir everything together and allow the meat to marinate for about an hour. Because of the marinade, the meat should keep very well for about three or four days in the refrigerator.

After the meat has marinated, soak some bamboo skewers in water so that they won't catch fire and burn when they go onto a hot grill. Then, put the meat onto the skewers, alternating the meat with red grapes. Add some oil to the skewered meat and grapes to keep them from sticking to the grill, and season them with salt. Then, grill the skewers for about eight minutes. After about four minutes, turn them. The grapes offer just a little bit of sweetness, which complements the exotic spices. Before serving the grilled pork and grapes, add a few drops of lemon juice.

Sauces—From Beurre Blanc to Béchamel
Lesson 13

The French built a culinary tradition that was all about technique—not about recipes or ingredients. Once a chef learned those techniques, it didn't matter where he or she went in the world, the technique would serve as a great culinary base. Sauces, such as béchamel and beurre blanc, are prominent in French food. In this lesson, you will learn about French mother sauces, Spanish romesco sauce, Chinese five-spice honey dip, and Thai curry.

The Evolution of French Sauces

About 150 years ago, French culinarians decided that the art of making French cuisine should be an honorable profession and that it needed to be more orderly, organized, and efficient. They even wanted to improve the realm of sauces and came up with a great plan to do so. They had the idea to make a series of mother sauces—which could be made in large quantities and stored very easily—that could be turned into a number of derivative sauces.

The Five Mother Sauces

The five mother sauces include espagnole, which is a brown sauce, and hollandaise, which is an emulsified sauce. A sauce called velouté, which translates as "velvety," is a sauce made from stock, and a sauce called béchamel, which is a white sauce, is a Lenten sauce that is made from milk instead of meat. Finally, there is a tomato sauce.

As an example, the mother sauce of brown sauces is the espagnole, or Spanish, sauce. If you add a reduction of red wine—especially bordeaux wine—to an espagnole sauce, you can turn it into a bordelaise sauce. In addition, the mother sauce hollandaise could be turned into a béarnaise sauce by making a reduction of tarragon, herbs, and vinegar.

Over the years, French sauces have continued to evolve, and the mother sauces have been left behind a little bit. French culinarians are now using lighter sauces—sauces with less flour in them—and sauces that are made from the pan drippings of pieces of cooked meat.

Béchamel Sauce

Shopping List

proportions to taste

butter
flour
whole milk, cold
onion piqué (onion, a bay
    leaf, and a few cloves)

salt
cayenne pepper
nutmeg

Béchamel is a French sauce that is especially consumed during the Lenten season on Fridays, when the consumption of meat is supposed to be avoided. It begins with a roux, which is butter and flour that are cooked together. The butter separates the grains of starch in the flour so that when you add it later to a sauce, it doesn't lump up. To make a roux, start by breaking up the butter and placing it in a warm pan. Melt the butter and cook the flour. You don't want the flour to brown, but the starch will gelatinize just a little bit and will start to feel a little bit sandy.

You need enough butter in the roux so that it's a semisolid and semiliquid, so use slightly more flour than butter. It should be similar to the consistency of tomato paste. Keep stirring the roux because you don't want it to burn. A béchamel is a white sauce, so you don't want the roux to be colored at all, but you do want to cook it long enough for the raw flavor to cook out of the flour. To check whether the roux is done, rub a little bit of it between your thumb and forefinger. It's hot, so be careful, but it should feel a little bit sandy; it shouldn't feel velvety the way flour feels.

When you add cold whole milk to the roux, it will begin to thicken almost immediately. The starch granules will begin to swell, and they will absorb the liquid. For this portion of the cooking, use a sauce whisk, which has a finer tip and heavier wire so that you can get into the corner of the pan. As you gradually stir in the milk, take advantage of the thickness of the mixture to break up any lumps and then introduce more liquid. Incrementally, the sauce will become looser and looser. Soon, you will find that the sauce walks the line between liquid and solid. Then, let it simmer for about 15 minutes, during which time it will tighten slightly, but it will also lose any raw flavor that is inherent in the flour.

As it is simmering, add a flavoring called an onion piqué, which involves an onion, a bay leaf, and a few cloves. After about 15 minutes, season it with salt. Instead of adding black pepper into this white sauce, add a little bit of cayenne pepper, which will spice the sauce without leaving any dark flecks in it. Also add a pinch of nutmeg to finish the béchamel.

Mornay Sauce

To turn the béchamel sauce into a mornay sauce, or cheese sauce, stir in a little bit of mustard and cheese, such as gruyère. You may discover that the flavor is bigger with the additional ingredients, so the sauce may need a slight adjustment to its seasoning. Add more salt, another pinch of cayenne, and a little bit more nutmeg if needed.

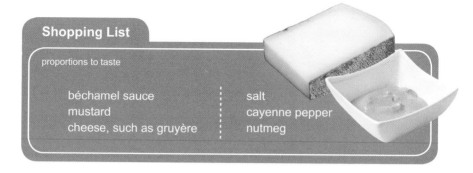
Repurposing Mornay Sauce

Once you have made mornay sauce, you can add it to cooked pasta to make macaroni and cheese. After adding quite a bit of this cheese sauce to the pasta, cover the top with some bread crumbs and just a little bit more grated cheese so that you get a nice gratin on the top. Add extra sauce to the pasta because it will be thirsty as it bakes. Then, put it into the oven. If it was at room temperature, bake the macaroni and cheese for about 30 to 35 minutes at 350 to 375 degrees, and it will come out bubbly, hot, and golden brown on the top.

Beurre Blanc

A more contemporary French sauce called beurre blanc is a white butter sauce. To make a beurre blanc, you need to start with a reduction. Add some white wine to a hot pan and then add some shallots and a few peppercorns to the wine. Then, add some vinegar, using about twice as much wine as vinegar. Add some lemon zest as well. Let the liquid in the pan reduce until it's nearly dry—à sec—and once it's reduced, strain out the solids and put it into another pan to build the beurre blanc.

After the liquid has reduced, bring the contents of the pan up to a boil. Then, turn the heat down, add butter—piece by piece—and season with salt. You want the butter to stay emulsified and creamy, so use cold butter. You don't want the butter to boil because boiling over time will make the sauce break, so you want the heat to be high enough that the butter is melting but not boiling. You want this mixture to become a thick, creamy sauce.

If you had started with red wine instead of white wine, you would have what is known as a beurre rouge, or red butter sauce. You could have even added citrus juice to your reduction and made a butter sauce that tasted of grapefruit, lime, or orange, for example.

Finally, taste and season the sauce. You might want to add more salt, but black pepper is probably not appropriate because it's a white sauce. Even white pepper might be a little too dark, so add just a pinch of cayenne pepper instead. This is a sauce, so it should taste a little sharp. Add some lemon juice to brighten it up. If the sauce coats the back of a spoon when you dip a spoon into it, that's indicative of a well-made sauce. French culinarians refer to the coating of the spoon as nappé.

Once the sauce is made, you need to make sure that it stays warm—but not too hot. In a restaurant, chefs might put it into a thermos to keep it hot. You can also keep it warm on the stove. Kept warm, the sauce will last very well for about an hour.

Serve the beurre blanc with a pan-fried chicken breast. Spoon some of the sauce on top of the chicken, letting it pool on the plate just a little bit. Sprinkle some fennel tops over the chicken as well.

Romesco Sauce

Shopping List

proportions to taste

peppers, roasted, peeled, and canned	olive oil
nuts	vinegar
garlic	cream
pimentón	salt
cayenne pepper	lemon juice
tomato paste	sherry vinegar
bread	

Romesco, which is very popular in Spain, is a simple sauce to make. Start by adding some canned peppers that have been roasted and peeled to a hot pan. This sauce is enriched with nuts—as are many sauces in the Mediterranean, such as pesto sauce. Add some nuts; garlic; and pimentón, which is a smoky paprika that is a Spanish specialty. It has a very smoky flavor, and a little bit goes a long way. If you want the sauce to be spicy, add just a little bit of cayenne pepper. Then, add some tomato paste.

To thicken the sauce, add a little bit of bread. In fact, the nuts and bread both provide the thickening and emulsification. Then, add olive oil and vinegar to the sauce. You will notice that it will become a very thick, creamy sauce. To the same pan, introduce a little bit of cream, which has a very powerful emulsion

in it. Then, strain it so that all of the solids stay behind. Taste the sauce and add any salt, cayenne, or pimentón that it might need. Let it sit for a few minutes.

After the sauce has had a chance to sit, taste it again, adding perhaps some more salt, a splash of lemon juice, or even some sherry vinegar. Some people characterize this sauce as the ketchup of Spain. It's great with grilled food—especially with grilled seafood and grilled vegetables.

Serve this rustic romesco with a grilled chicken breast. Spoon some of the sauce next to the chicken and sprinkle a little bit of parsley over the whole thing. A side of grilled vegetables will taste just as good with the romesco as the chicken does.

Five-Spice Honey Dip

Shopping List

proportions to taste

honey
ginger
Chinese five spice

soy sauce
rice wine vinegar

To make this Asian sauce, put some honey into a bowl and then add ginger and Chinese five spice, which is a common Asian blend that you can buy at the market. Stir the contents of the bowl together and then add soy sauce, which will create a balance between the sweetness of the honey and the salty, savory flavor of the soy. In addition, the ginger and Chinese five spice will accentuate the aroma of the honey. To introduce some acidity to this mixture, add some rice wine vinegar.

This sauce is great over grilled food, such as a piece of grilled salmon. It is also delicious over vegetables. You can keep this sauce in your refrigerator in a little mason jar for about two months or longer.

Thai Green Curry

Shopping List

proportions to taste

oil
curry paste
pork tenderloin, cut
coconut milk
fish sauce
sugar

vegetables, such as red peppers, red tomatoes, yellow peppers, and snow peas, cut
chiles
basil leaves
tomatoes
rice, precooked

When you know how to make either Thai green curry paste, yellow curry paste, or red curry paste, you know how to make them all. Begin with a hot pan and a little bit of oil. When you make a Thai curry, don't use more than one or two tablespoons of curry paste per 14-ounce can of coconut milk—depending on how spicy you like your curry.

Wake up the flavors of the curry paste by adding it to the hot pan; almost immediately, it becomes really aromatic. You can also add some cut pork tenderloin to the pan, coating it with the curry paste. Pork tenderloin is a fairly tender cut of meat, so it doesn't take much cooking. Then, add coconut milk to the pan. You will notice that the color of the curry paste will turn the coconut milk a little dark.

Season the liquid with fish sauce, which should be added as if it were salt, and then taste it. When it tastes salty enough, temper the saltiness with a little bit of sugar. Add more coconut milk if it is too spicy. Then, add a selection of vegetables, such as red peppers, red tomatoes, yellow peppers, and snow peas. Cut the vegetables before adding them to the pan. Also add some chiles. If you like your curry hot, you can add extra chiles, but be careful not to add too many. At the end, add a bunch of basil leaves and some tomatoes.

Put the curry in a bowl with precooked rice. This dish tastes so delicious and fresh—and it is so easy and quick to make—that it might be a go-to meal for you.

Grains and Legumes—
Cooking for Great Flavor
Lesson 14

Almost every culture in the world consumes some combination of grains and legumes because that combination is a nutritional powerhouse. Together, grains and legumes will give you complete protein, especially in the absence of abundant meat. There are all kinds of grains—including oats, wheat, rye, barley, sorghum, wild rice, quinoa, and teff—that serve as fuel for the human body. Legumes include peas and beans and provide additional health benefits. In this lesson, you will learn some techniques for cooking various grains and legumes that you can put to the test in your kitchen.

Soaking and Cooking Beans

Before cooking any type of beans, spread them out on a sheet pan, or cookie sheet. Beans are an agricultural product that are minimally processed, so before cooking beans, you should check to see if there are any little pieces of dirt or even a few stones that are mixed in with your beans. You may also see some old or broken beans, which can be discarded.

After examining them, put the beans into a bowl. They are now ready to be washed and then soaked. They should be soaked overnight in abundant water, using 2 to 3 times as much water as beans. It is best to put them in the refrigerator because beans still represent protein and, therefore, shouldn't sit out at room temperature.

After the beans have soaked, put them into a pot—along with the water they soaked in. Make sure that the beans are covered by about a half an inch to an inch of water. Turn on the heat and begin cooking them. Flavor the beans with some herbs and garlic. You might choose to flavor them with a branch of sage, but also add some

The Quick-Soak Method

If you don't have enough time to let beans soak overnight before cooking them, put the beans into a pot, cover them with abundant water, bring them up to a boil, and boil them for a few minutes. Then, turn off the heat and let them sit for about an hour before you carry on with your cooking. However, try not to use this method every time. The beans will be fuller and less likely to break apart when you cook them if they are able to soak and rehydrate slowly overnight.

rosemary and a few bay leaves. The beans will absorb the flavor of the garlic and herbs as they cook.

After the beans have cooked for about an hour, they should be done cooking. If the beans have been cooking for more than an hour and don't seem to be done, the problem could be simply that they are old beans—that they are extra dry and need more time to cook. More likely, if you added salt to the beans too early in the cooking process, that could keep them from getting tender. However, if you haven't added salt, then your water is probably hard, and the extra acidity from the hard water is keeping the beans from cooking to tenderness.

To neutralize the acidity, add a pinch of baking soda to the pot. Baking soda reacts to acidity, so you will see it start to bubble up if you are working with very hard water. Don't add a lot of baking soda to the water because, ultimately, it can make the beans fall apart and taste soapy. Just test to see if the acidity is the issue with a pinch of baking soda, and if you see a response, then add no more than a quarter of a teaspoon of baking soda to the water.

Once the beans are cooked and tender, then you can add salt, which will help them hold their shape. If you are using white beans, don't use black pepper; instead, add some pepper flakes, which will give a little fleck of color. The starch in the beans gives a very distinctive body to the cooking liquid. Because beans should be stored in liquid, store them—along with the cooking liquid—in a plastic container in the refrigerator or freezer.

Evaluating Doneness

After beans have cooked for about an hour, depending on the type of bean, they will have swollen to about twice the size they were when they were raw. To determine whether the beans are done cooking, take a bean out of the pot, put it between your thumb and forefinger, and smear it. If it feels grainy or coarse—or anything but velvety smooth—the beans are not cooked yet. You can also pop it in your mouth, and if it feels dry, sandy, grainy, or chalky, then the beans that are not yet fully cooked.

Types of Rice

Short-grain rice is the type of rice that is used in sushi and risotto. Short-grain rice is about twice as long as it is fat. When it cooks, the starch becomes very sticky. Medium-grain rice is about three times as long as it is fat, and when it is cooked, it is significantly less sticky than short-grain rice. Long-grain rice is about five times as long as it is fat, and when it cooks, it becomes very soft and fluffy—the grains don't stick together at all.

Whole grain rice has added nutrition, but because of the bran and fiber that it contains, it takes longer to cook than white rice. If white rice cooks in about 15 minutes, then whole grain rice takes nearly 45 minutes. Quinoa is an example of a whole grain that cooks very quickly. Because it is so small, it cooks in about 15 minutes even though it contains bran and fiber.

Rice Pilaf

Shopping List

proportions to taste

basmati rice	salt
chicken stock	butter
thyme	onions, sautéed
bay leaves	oil
red pepper flakes	

Rice-Cooking Tip

If you don't know how much liquid that a particular grain should cook in, you can also cook grains in water the way you might cook pasta. You probably won't need as much water, but cover the grains with abundant liquid in a pot and then turn the heat on and cook them. When the grains are done cooking, you can simply pour out the excess liquid, repurposing it by adding it to a soup, for example. As the grains cook, flavor them in whatever way you choose. Just remember that different grains take different amounts of time to cook.

Rice pilaf is a great technique for keeping rice loose and fluffy. Start to finish, this method of cooking rice takes about 20 minutes. Rice pilaf involves cooking the grain in a measured amount of liquid, so you need to know which grain you are beginning with in order to measure the correct amount of liquid. For example, basmati rice uses about one part rice to about one and a half to one and three-quarters parts liquid.

To cook basmati rice, add to a pot the appropriate amount of liquid—which can be water, chicken stock, or even vegetable stock—and some basmati rice. For this dish, use chicken stock. As flavorings, add a branch of thyme, a few bay leaves, and a pinch of pepper flakes. Don't use black pepper with rice like this because if you do, you will see little black specks against something that is basically white.

Finally, add salt as if you were seasoning a soup; the liquid should taste like a well-seasoned broth.

Stir everything to make sure the rice isn't sticking together and bring the liquid up to a boil. Then, reduce the heat so that the liquid maintains a simmer and continue to cook the rice with a tight-fitting lid over the pot. After about 17 or 18 minutes, all of the moisture should be absorbed, and the rice should be tender. At that point, you can turn the heat off. Let the rice sit for about five minutes because cooked rice can be delicate. You don't want to manipulate it too much; otherwise, you'll break up the grains.

If the rice is properly cooked, there shouldn't be any excess liquid that pours to the side of the pot when you tilt it. All of the liquid should have been absorbed by the rice. If you taste the rice, it should be tender and properly seasoned. After letting the rice rest, add a little bit of butter to flavor it. Grab a fork and fluff the rice very gently; don't stir it with a spoon, and don't be too aggressive. Along the way, you may find the remnants of the thyme and bay leaves, which can be removed before serving.

In a heated pan, sauté some onions in oil until they turn translucent. Then, add the rice to the pan and coat the grains with the flavorful fat that is already

inherent in the pan. Coat each grain in the oil, which will protect it from sticking to other grains of rice. As you cook the rice, the outside starch on each grain of rice will gelatinize with the heat and will firmly coat each grain so that it doesn't stick to its neighbor. You will notice that the rice will change from being translucent to being slightly white and chalky. After about a minute and a half of cooking, the rice may begin to brown just a little bit, and you will notice a toasty, nutty aroma.

Grain Medley

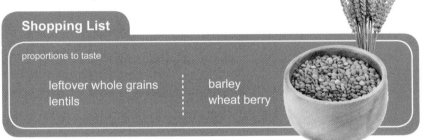

Shopping List

proportions to taste

| leftover whole grains | barley |
| lentils | wheat berry |

Because whole grains take a lot of time to cook, you can make extra and can keep the leftovers in the refrigerator or freezer. Then, when you are ready to use them, add other cooked grains—such as lentils, barley, and wheat berry—to the whole grain leftovers, resulting in a nutritional powerhouse combination of grains and legumes. Dishes that take advantage of this combination have a complex flavor and a wonderful visual texture.

Mushroom Risotto

Risotto is a preparation that takes advantage of the starch in short-grain rice and leverages it so that it turns into a creamy sauce. Start to finish, a risotto takes about 18 minutes to prepare, but it demands your attention throughout the process—it's not something that you can make ahead of time. To make mushroom risotto, start by dicing and sautéing a nice selection of mushrooms, such as shitake, wild, and trumpet royale mushrooms.

When you make a risotto, you can think of it as having very distinct parts. First, there's a foundation of flavor. In this case, the foundation is pancetta with garlic and onions. Second, there's the rice that goes into the pan and the broth that it cooks in, which is seasoned chicken stock. You should use about four times as much stock as rice. Finally, there's a garnish, which is the mushrooms.

Once the pan is hot, add oil. Once you start to see smoke, add the mushrooms so that the oil doesn't burn. Nothing enhances the flavor of mushrooms like a high-heat sear; the caramelization that occurs brings out a delicious meatiness in the mushrooms. As soon as you see some color on the mushrooms and they are just beginning to get tender, add the garlic to the pan. Then, introduce some thyme and a splash of white wine. Finally, season the mushrooms with salt and pepper. When the mushrooms are done cooking, take them off the heat and set them aside while you make the risotto.

To make the risotto, start with the foundational flavor. Add some pancetta to a pan, rendering the fat out of it and browning it just a little bit. If you dice or mince the pancetta into very fine pieces of meat, it will cook very quickly. Then, add some onions to the pan and let them cook along with the pancetta.

If you see the meat leaving behind a little bit of a residue on the bottom of the pan, don't let it burn. Introduce a tiny amount of liquid and clean the bottom of the pan by scraping the residue off of the bottom to avoid having burnt flavors in your risotto. After the pancetta and onions have had some time to cook, add some garlic and thyme.

Next, add some short-grain Arborio rice to the pan, coating it in flavorful fat. The first addition of liquid is wine. Because risotto celebrates the stickiness of the starch that is found in the rice, you want to tease the starch out of the grain by adding small amounts of liquid and then

Mushroom Tips

Using a selection of mushrooms in a risotto gives it a depth of flavor and complexity that wouldn't result form just a single type of mushroom. In addition, if you are using dried mushrooms, you can rehydrate them in liquid, which could then become part of the broth that you cook the risotto in.

stirring almost constantly to make a creamy sauce. Add about a half to three-quarters of a cup of wine. Cook this preparation at a low temperature so that it maintains a simmer.

After the wine has been absorbed, incrementally add seasoned broth that is already hot so that you don't have to wait for it to come up to temperature. If you add too much liquid at once, the texture of the grain becomes spoiled. Instead, you want to tease the starch out of the rice by stirring it and adding liquid incrementally. Continuously monitor the texture of your risotto because if you add too much liquid, it will be soupy, and if you don't add enough liquid, it will be dry. Before a new addition of liquid, let the rice become almost dry. Toward the end of the cooking, a creamy sauce begins to take shape.

After about 15 minutes, taste a grain of rice to make sure that it is starting to get tender. If it's not ready, there will be a chalky, hard center to each grain. You need to continue to cook until each grain is firm but tender. At that point, you can add the mushrooms—the garniture—to the risotto.

Traditionally, risotto is finished with butter and cheese, so add a knob of butter and grate some cheese into it and on top of it. Do this before you evaluate the finished seasoning because the richness and the salty, savory flavor of the cheese will impact the finished dish. At this point, don't stir the rice too aggressively; instead, fold the final ingredients in. You want a preparation that holds its shape on a spoon without running off. Finally, stir in some salt, pepper, chives, and parsley.

Salads from the Cold Kitchen

Lesson 15

If you are like other fledgling cooks, then you will first seek to master the most complicated recipes as proof of your burgeoning skills. Then, as you make more progress, you will come to realize that simplicity is the hallmark of great cooking. You search for great ingredients; honor their intrinsic flavor, texture, and color; and do what you can to stay out of the way of their goodness. Salads should contain ingredients that are so good that you want to do what you can to showcase them with the minimum amount of fuss and manipulation.

Bistro Salad with Butter Lettuce and Fine Herbs

Shopping List

proportions to taste

butter lettuce, washed	Dijon mustard
flat-leaf parsley, coarsely chopped	shallots
chives, chopped	salt
tarragon, cut	ground black pepper
chervil or fennel tops	vinegar
	oil

On the outside of a head of lettuce are wrapper leaves, which protect the lettuce, so they are often a little bit bruised and should be discarded. When you cut the core out of lettuce, try to be gentle; otherwise, it'll get bruised. Once the core is out, you can separate it into leaves. Lettuce is somewhere between 90 and 95 percent water, so even a small loss in moisture means that it becomes limp and begins to wilt. If your lettuce loses moisture, you can help the lettuce crisp up again by soaking it in ice water.

If you are making a salad for dinner, wash the lettuce in a bowl of very cold water and then blot it dry with towels or spin it dry in a salad spinner. Make sure that you lift the lettuce from the water—not dump the lettuce with the dirty water into a colander—so that any dirt that was on this lettuce, which has fallen to the bottom, will stay on the bottom. Then, put the lettuce in the refrigerator for about an hour, at which point it will be fresh and crisp.

A traditional bistro salad uses butter lettuce, which is a mild green. In addition to butter lettuce, this salad contains a nice selection of fine herbs—which are delicate and tender—such as parsley, tarragon, chervil, and chives. First, chop some flat-leaf parsley fairly coarsely and chop some chives as well. Then, strip the leaves from some tarragon, which has a wonderful anise flavor, and cut them into large pieces. Finally, pluck some chervil from its stem. This delicate herb has a mild and sweet anise flavor that is not nearly as strong as that of tarragon. If you can't find chervil, use fennel tops, which also have a mild anise flavor.

The Oil-to-Vinegar Ratio

Traditionally, vinaigrette salad dressings should contain one part vinegar to three parts oil, but you can vary that proportion if you invest in some good-quality oil and want the oil to play a starring role. In that case, you might want to use four or even five parts of oil to one part of vinegar. In fact, an old adage in French cooking states that when you are making a salad, you want to be a madman with the whip, a spendthrift with the oil, and a miser with the vinegar.

To make the dressing for this salad, start by adding Dijon mustard, which will act as an emulsifier to hold together oil and vinegar, to a bowl. Add some shallots and some salt and pepper as well. Then, add vinegar and oil in the standard proportion of one part vinegar to three parts oil, drizzling the oil in little by little while you whip it all together. If the mixture ever starts looking greasy, don't add the oil as quickly as you have been. Another way to mix this dressing is to put all of the ingredients into a canning jar with a lid and shake it vigorously to emulsify it.

Because lettuce is mostly made up of water, you need a fairly strong vinaigrette to make a lot of lettuce taste delicious. If the vinaigrette tastes great right off the spoon, chances are that it is not assertive enough. If it bites a little bit, then you're on the right track. When the vinaigrette is ready, lightly dress the lettuce and herbs with the vinaigrette, barely coating the lettuce.

Add all of the herbs to a bowl with the washed butter lettuce, which should be placed in the bowl with whole leaves instead of cutting or tearing the leaves. Start by placing some of the larger leaves on the bottom of the bowl, in effect, to rebuild the head of lettuce. Let the color of the leaves guide you; start with the darker leaves and build up to the lighter leaves. Top the salad with some more of the delicate chervil that is undressed so that it doesn't mat together.

Endive Blue Cheese Salad with Walnuts

Shopping List

proportions to taste

Belgian endive, washed
Roquefort cheese
tarragon
lemon juice
salt
ground black pepper

oils, such as olive oil, walnut oil, and toasted nut oil
walnuts, toasted and coarsely chopped

To make a salad with Belgian endive, which is a bitter green, the dressing has to be very assertive to stand up to the bitterness of the greens. Therefore, you are going to use toasted walnuts and Roquefort cheese, a sheep's milk cheese that has plenty of flavor. In fact, the dressing starts with some cheese that is broken into pieces. Then, add some tarragon, lemon juice, salt, and pepper.

Next, add a combination of oils, such as a fairly mild olive oil, walnut oil, and toasted nut oil. Because it is perishable, once you open a container of toasted nut oil, it should be stored in the refrigerator. Also, buy it in small quantities so that you can use it all within a few months. When you stir everything together, the cheese will break down to form an emulsified, creamy dressing, but you still want to

Storing Leafy Greens

In general, when storing lettuces or leafy greens, you should be aware that there are fruits that give off a hormone known as ethylene gas, which makes leafy greens turn brown. If you have two drawers in your refrigerator for produce, put fruit in one and leafy greens in the other to prevent the leafy greens from turning brown.

leave a few big chunks of cheese intact. Coarsely chop some walnuts and add them to the dressing.

Take the end off of the endive and discard it. Then, you can either break the endive apart into whole leaves or you can cut it; either way, make sure to remove the core that runs down the center. The leaves can begin to brown if you cut the endive too early in the process of creating the salad. The leaves brown because certain enzymes become exposed to the air and begin to turn color—just the way an apple might turn color once you cut it. Washing the lettuce in cold water, however, washes some of the enzymes away from the surface so that browning becomes less of an issue.

To assemble the salad, start by gently putting the greens into a bowl. If you have any whole leaves that were not cut, put those in the bottom of the bowl and then make a mound with the endive that was cut. Then, add the dressing to the salad. The cheese and walnuts tend to sink to the bottom of the dressing, so when you pour the dressing over the endive, they become the garnish on top of the salad.

Vietnamese Salad Rolls

Vietnamese salad rolls are great appetizers, or hors d'oeuvres, because they are like handheld, interactive salads. They are served with a dipping sauce that is fat free. If you want the salad rolls to taste spicy, use a lot of dipping sauce, but if you don't want them to taste spicy, use only a little sauce.

The dressing for these salad rolls is called *nouc cham*, and to make it, start by finely cutting some Thai bird chiles, which are very spicy. If the chiles are small, seeding them and cutting the ribs out of them is not very practical. About 60 percent of the heat of a chili is in the ribs of that chili, 20 percent is in the seeds, and the last 20 percent is in the flesh.

Add the chiles and some garlic to a bowl. Then, add fish sauce, which is a condiment from Southeast Asia that has a wonderful savory flavor but smells very fishy. Before adding fish sauce to any dish, taste it because you will find that it is very salty, and you want to find the balance between the saltiness of

the fish sauce and sugar. Then, add sugar until you can taste sweetness and saltiness—but neither should predominate.

Next, brighten the flavor with some acidic lime juice. Then, mix everything together, making sure that all the sugar is dissolved. If the dipping sauce is too intense, thin it out by adding a little bit of water. As a garnish, thinly slice some carrots.

Rice noodles, or rice vermicelli, are noodles that are made by taking a batter of rice flour and water and extruding it into boiling water. The noodles are cooked and then are dried later. They take about four minutes to cook when you are ready to make them. Don't confuse rice noodles with bean threads, or cellophane noodles, which are perfectly clear when they cook.

Rice papers are also made with a batter of rice flour and water, but they are spread over a piece of linen that is stretched over the top of a boiling pot. As the steam passes through the linen, it cooks the crepe that rests on top. When it is cooked, it is peeled off and very delicately placed onto a bamboo mat in the sun to dry. If you look carefully, you can see the design left behind by the bamboo mat that it dried on. Because rice papers have already been cooked, you simply need to rehydrate them by putting them into warm water.

On a cutting board, spread out a dampened piece of a cheesecloth or a kitchen towel to prevent the rice papers from sitting in water, which can cause them to oversoften and tear. You want the rice papers to begin to soften and lose their leathery feel, and they can continue softening on the damp cloth. Once the rice papers become flexible, but not soft, then you can take them out of the warm water, and they will finish rehydrating on the cutting board. Little by little, the rice papers will absorb all of the surface moisture and become a little bit sticky—but this takes time.

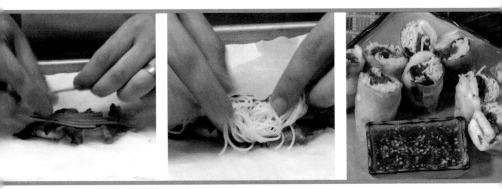

To build the salad rolls, start with something brightly colored, such as a lettuce leaf. Put the lettuce leaf at the bottom third of the rice paper and make sure that you leave behind the hard ribs. You only need the tender lettuce. Think about color as you continue building your salad rolls, alternating bright colors with muted ones. After adding the lettuce, add some rice noodles on top of the lettuce. Then, add some julienned carrots that have been very quickly blanched so that they are not too hard. Fresh herbs are a big part of Vietnamese food, so lay some basil leaves, mint leaves, and cilantro on top of the carrots. Make sure that you are using good-quality herbs in this dish.

Finally, tightly roll the rice paper up once, compacting the filling. Then, add the shrimp—with its colorful side on the outside—and continue rolling the rice paper up. When you get to the thickest part, fold the edges in; you'll notice that the edges stick to themselves pretty easily. Make sure not to use too much filling because the rice paper can tear. If one of the rice papers tears, which is especially problematic if it has been handled too aggressively, just replace it with a new rice paper and start all over again.

These salad rolls can be stored at room temperature, but if you have to refrigerate them, cover them with a damp towel so that the rice papers don't begin to dry out.

Segmenting an Orange

To take the segments out of an orange, cut the top and bottom of the orange off so that it sits flat on a cutting board. Use your knife to peel away the rind, exposing the meat of the orange. Then, cut between two membranes to remove the first segment. After you have removed the first segment, cut between the next two membranes on one side, and the membrane should peel away from the other side.

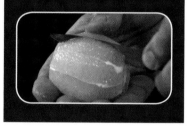

When you are ready to serve the salad rolls, cut them straight across because if you cut them on a diagonal, very often they will come undone. Sit them up on one end so that you can see the filling. The dipping sauce is an integral part of this dish, so make sure that your guests realize that they should dip the salad rolls into the dipping sauce.

Chicken, Shrimp, and Fruit Salad

Salad doesn't have to be something that comes before an entrée—it can be an entrée—and this delicious Southeast Asian salad is great for a light lunch or even a light dinner.

Shopping List

proportions to taste

orange segments, seedless
green apples, diced
red grapes, seedless, cut in half
green grapes, seedless, cut in half
chicken, poached, shredded
shrimp
serrano pepper
cilantro, chopped

peanuts, dry-roasted
shallots, sliced, fried
garlic, sliced, fried
lime juice
sugar
salt

To make this chicken, shrimp, and fruit salad, start with seedless orange segments, diced green apples, and seedless red and green grapes that have been cut in half. You will also need some poached chicken that has been shredded and some shrimp as well.

Many Southeast Asian dressings do not contain any oil, and this particular salad dressing is no exception. To make the fat-free dressing for this salad, start with some serrano chili peppers. Remove the seeds and ribs of the peppers if you want to tone down the spiciness of this dish. Then, add some chopped cilantro and dry-roasted peanuts. Next, gently fry some sliced shallots and garlic at about 250 degrees and then brown them before adding them to the mixture. Add lime juice and balance the acidity of the lime juice with sugar. Then, add salt.

Once the dressing is ready, combine the chicken, shrimp, and fruit in a bowl and then add the dressing. If you are going to keep this salad for a while, gather all of the ingredients together, but do not dress it until just before you are ready to serve it.

Eggs—From the Classic to the Contemporary
Lesson 16

Cooking eggs can teach you a lot about cooking in general. If cooking is the application of heat to food, then eggs—as a particularly delicate food—will tell you if you get it right or if you get it wrong. In this lesson, you will learn how to prepare eggs in various ways, including hard-boiled, poached, and scrambled eggs. Specifically, you will learn how to make deviled eggs, eggs benedict, and even a rolled omelet filled with ratatouille.

Tips for Buying Eggs

When you go to the store to buy eggs, check the expiration date on the container of eggs and buy as far into the future as you can. Freshness is the most important quality to look for. Sometimes eggs are graded, but take the grading with a grain of salt. Grading is done when the eggs are packed, and a good-quality egg doesn't mean anything unless it's been handled properly on its way to the store.

Egg Color

The color of an egg is not an indication of quality; instead, it is an indication of breed.

Once you have chosen a carton of eggs, open it and make sure that none of the eggs are cracked or broken because they can start to spoil. If you notice that there are some cracked or broken eggs when you get home, it's safest to just discard them. As soon as you get home, put the eggs directly into the refrigerator.

Hard-Boiled Eggs

To hard-boil eggs, start with enough water in a pot so that the eggs are covered by at least two inches of water, and turn the heat up on the stove. While the water is still cool, lower the eggs into the water, being careful not to crack the eggs when you put them in. Then, bring the water up to a boil. As soon as the water starts to boil, turn the heat down as low as you can and start a timer. For large eggs, take them out after 12 minutes and then put them into ice water to stop the cooking.

For an extra-large egg, you might want to wait about 14 minutes to take the eggs out of the pot; for a medium egg, you might want to wait only 10 minutes.

In terms of quality, the size doesn't really matter, but many recipes will usually call for a large or an extra-large egg.

When you are ready to peel the eggs, do it at the sink and let the water from the faucet flow between the shell and the egg—they should separate pretty easily. Fresh eggs are sometimes difficult to peel. Try closing your eyes and feeling for pieces of shells; you may not see them because both the shell and the egg are white, but you'll feel them.

Deviled Eggs

Shopping List

proportions to taste

hard-boiled eggs, cut in half	Worcestershire sauce
mayonnaise	basil
salt	tomato, chopped
Tabasco sauce	horseradish
mustard	chives

To make deviled eggs, cut some hard-boiled eggs in half with a sharp knife. The yolk should be set but still moist, and the white should be set but not rubbery. In contrast, an overcooked hard-boiled egg is very dry and rubbery. If you don't like that little bit of moisture, then add an extra minute to the cooking time, and if you want your eggs to be a little bit more moist, then subtract a minute.

Start by slipping the yolks out of the whites. Make sure not to break the whites because they will be the container that holds the filling. Once you have removed all of the yolks and placed them into a bowl, mix them with some mayonnaise until the yolks have broken down. You want the mixture to have a creamy consistency; you don't want it to be too dry.

The Spin Test: Hard-Boiled versus Raw Eggs

It's sometimes difficult to distinguish between hard-boiled eggs and raw eggs that are sitting in your refrigerator. If you pick up an egg and spin it on the counter, if it's hard-boiled, it will spin really well because both the white and the yolk are firm on the inside. However, if you try to spin a raw egg, it will not spin at all.

Season the mixture with a little salt—but not pepper. Small flecks of black pepper make the yolk mixture less attractive. Instead, add some Tabasco sauce, which will give the peppery flavor that you want without the small flecks. Then, stir in some mustard to cut through the richness of this preparation. If you like a savory flavor, you can add a splash of Worcestershire sauce. If you want to, you can add other herbs, such as basil, or even some chopped up tomato. Some people add horseradish as well.

Cooking Eggs

You should have a special pan for cooking eggs that is nonstick and is used only for eggs. You should take really good care of pans like these, including washing them by hand so that the nonstick coating stays in great shape.

You don't have to pipe the filling into the eggs; instead, you can take a little spoonful of the filling and spoon it into the eggs. Alternately, you can put all of the filling into a ziplock bag and cut the tip off of the bag to use it as a pastry bag and pipe in the filling. If you have a proper pastry bag and you like a fluted appearance, you can put a star tip in the pastry bag and pipe the filling. Finally, sprinkle some chives on top to add some contrasting color. Your eggs should either go right into the refrigerator or onto a plate to be served.

Eggs Benedict and Hollandaise Sauce

To make eggs benedict, you can start by making hollandaise sauce, which needs a flavorful reduction. First, add about three tablespoons of water and three tablespoons of vinegar to a pan. Then, add some minced shallots and two or three peppercorns. Cook over the heat until it is reduced by half of its original volume, which won't take very long. After it is reduced, strain the reduction into a bowl so that the sauce won't be chunky with shallots and peppercorns.

Next, you need some egg yolks. To separate an egg into its yolk and whites, crack the egg and pull the shell apart over a bowl. The whites will spill out first, and then you have to transfer the yolk back and forth between the two shells very carefully until all of the whites have spilled out. Once you have done this three times, transfer the yolks into a large stainless-steel bowl. For each of the yolks, add about a tablespoon of water to the bowl.

Set up a bain-marie bath, which is a hot-water bath in which the vapors coming off of the heated water (which is at a simmer—not boiling hard) in a pot heat the contents of a smaller pot that is placed in the bath. This will gently heat the bottom of the bowl containing the egg yolks.

Once you add the bowl to the bain-marie, you want to whip the egg yolks constantly so that they don't get cooked—in other words, you want them to stay nice and creamy. As you whip them, you'll discover that they become really thick and frothy. In fact, they will probably quadruple in volume. Eventually, you will notice that as the whip passes through the mixture, you will be able to see streaks of the bottom of the bowl. That is how you know that you are done whipping. If you use a thermometer, you want the egg yolks to be cooked to about 165 degrees. Start to finish, this will probably take about three minutes.

Once the egg yolks are fully whipped, slowly add hot clarified butter to make an emulsion, which is when two things that don't normally like to mix are mixed together. There are two phases of an emulsion: a continuous phase and a disbursed phase. The egg yolk mixture is in a continuous phase until it is disbursed with fat, or clarified butter.

When you start to establish an emulsion, you want to add the butter (or oil) very slowly—drop by drop—while you whip. The clue that your emulsion is beginning to form is that it will immediately start to thicken, at which point you can be a little

Keeping Hollandaise Warm

Hollandaise sauce is a bit problematic because it has butter in it. If it gets cold, the butter will congeal, and the sauce will separate into eggs and butter. If it gets too warm, the eggs will turn into scrambled eggs, and the sauce will separate into scrambled eggs and butter. To avoid these situations, you need to keep it warm—but not hot. If you need to keep it warm for a long time, a thermos is a great way to do so.

123

more cavalier and add the butter slightly more quickly. For each egg yolk, add about two ounces of clarified butter.

At no point should the mixture look anything but creamy. If it starts looking oily, then you are probably adding the butter too quickly. If you add any more than two ounces of butter per yolk, you might discover that the resulting hollandaise tastes dry. Alternatively, if you add any less than two ounces of butter per yolk, you might find that the egg yolk coats your mouth too completely—in which case you should add a little bit more butter.

While you're adding butter, you should be whipping. When you're done adding butter, you can stop whipping, but it still needs to be seasoned. Because the hollandaise is so thick, it would be very difficult to taste the flavor of pepper if you were to add it, so use a few drops of Tabasco sauce instead.

The sauce also needs salt, but in a thick sauce like hollandaise, it is sometimes difficult for salt to dissolve. When you add salt, also add a little bit of lemon juice to help the salt begin to dissolve. The lemon cuts through the richness of the butter and egg yolk. If it's already too tart and you can't add more lemon juice, then a little bit of water can be added as well. However, the sauce will start to become thin if you add too much water.

Eggs benedict is a dish that involves poached eggs. To poach an egg, fill a sautoir with water that is deep enough to cover an egg. Usually when poaching, add a little bit of acid to the water in the form of wine, vinegar, or lemon juice. The acid changes the pH and helps the protein coagulate more quickly. You don't want your eggs to be colored, so use a distilled vinegar, adding a tablespoon or two per quart of liquid.

Recall that poaching takes place at about 160 degrees. When you see steam coming off the top of the water, it's at about 160 degrees, but there will also be a few bubbles on the bottom of the pan that will lift the egg up and keep it off of the bottom. Once you see those bubbles, take an egg and crack it into a coffee cup, which will give you a handle to hold on to when you lower the egg into the liquid. As you lower the egg, let the hot water flow into the cup and gently tip the egg out against the side of the pan where you see some bubbles. Then, bring the white part of the egg up and over the top of the yolk. Try not to manipulate the egg too much while it is cooking.

Start to finish, a poached egg at about 160 degrees will take about three minutes. The first sign that it is on its way to being done is that the white will begin to set on the outside and turn opaque, but it would still be very loose if you were to try to manipulate it. Later, you will see that the white has cooked all the way through to the yolk, and when you manipulate it, it will be firm enough to kind of hold its shape—albeit gently.

Once you have decided that the egg is firm but the yolk is still soft, you can take the egg out of the water using a spoon or a skimmer that is perforated to drain the excess moisture off. Cover a plate with a paper towel and slide the egg onto it. Then, trim the excess white around the poached egg and gently transfer it over to a toasted english muffin that you have added a slice of ham to. Stir the hollandaise to loosen slightly and spoon it over the hot egg. Finally, add chives as a garnish. Start to finish, it takes about 15 minutes to make eggs benedict.

Scrambled Eggs

Shopping List

proportions to taste

eggs	ground black pepper
whole butter	chives
salt	cream

To make scrambled eggs, start by cracking eggs into a bowl, mixing them just to break up their structure a little bit—just until you no longer see the distinct whites and yolks separate from one another.

When cooking eggs, always use a nonstick pan. However, even with a nonstick pan, you also need to use some sort of fat. For scrambled eggs, use whole butter, which burns at a relatively low temperature (around 250 degrees).

First, you want to get the butter hot and up to temperature—but no hotter than it can tolerate. When you see some sizzling in the pan, that's the water cooking out of the butter. As soon as the water has left the pan, you can run into problems with the butter burning, so have your food ready to go in the pan at that point.

The eggs will cook quickly if your pan is preheated. Once it is preheated, use a ladle to add some eggs to it. Season the eggs with salt, pepper, and some chives. Turn the heat up a little bit to move the cooking along. To make your eggs a little bit richer, add a tablespoon of cream for each egg. That will keep your eggs soft and moist.

When you notice the eggs starting to turn to gentle, soft curds, turn the heat down and keep the eggs moving around the pan with a spatula. Your goal is not to have a dry, curdy mess, but to have gentle curds that are nice and moist. As the eggs get closer and closer to being done, pull the pan off the heat and use the residual heat that's left in the pan to finish cooking them.

Ratatouille Omelet

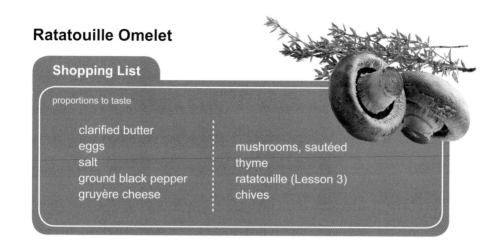

Shopping List

proportions to taste

clarified butter
eggs
salt
ground black pepper
gruyère cheese

mushrooms, sautéed
thyme
ratatouille (Lesson 3)
chives

To make an omelet, add clarified butter to a hot pan; add enough to cover the bottom of the pan. Once the pan is sizzling, the pan is hot and ready for you to add the eggs. Use a silicon spatula to keep the eggs moving around the pan, and add a little salt and pepper.

When the eggs are almost set, stop stirring to allow the scrambled eggs on the bottom of the pan to actually set. Pull the pan off the heat for just a second so that you can sprinkle some gruyère cheese into the omelet. Add some sautéed mushrooms with thyme to add some flavor. Put the pan back on the heat and see if the omelet slides free from the bottom of the pan when you knock the side of the pan.

Use your spatula to fold one-third of the omelet over on itself. Then, knock the omelet close to the edge of the pan and carefully roll it over onto the following third while letting it slide down onto a plate.

Instead of vegetables, use ratatouille as a filling for your omelet by cutting an opening into the omelet with a knife and spreading it open a little. Then, spoon the ratatouille into the opening of the omelet. Top it with some chives.

Soups from around the World

Lesson 17

Soup has been around for as long as there have been pots to cook soup in. Soup speaks to the human soul: It warms us up when the weather is cold, cools us down when the weather is hot, fills us up when we're ravenously hungry, and offers ready nutrition for a weak or timid appetite. Every culture has a soup that defines the culture and the people who eat it. For example, borscht, miso soup, chowder, goulash, and onion soup are all national soups, which is the subject of this lesson.

Tom Kha Gai

Shopping List

proportions to taste

coconut milk, canned	sugar
shallots, chopped	chicken, cut small
garlic, chopped	kaffir lime leaves or lime zest
lemongrass, chopped	white button mushrooms, thinly sliced
galangal, sliced	tomato concassé
sambal oelek	lime juice
chicken stock	cilantro
fish sauce	

The national soup of Thailand, tom kha gai, is a chicken soup that is made with coconut milk. To make it, start by turning the heat of the stove on. Instead of using canola or peanut oil, try using the coconut fat that sits on the top of a can of coconut milk. It is almost pure fat, with only a little bit of moisture. Add it to a hot pan and cook it until it breaks; you want the fat to come out of the coconut milk so that you can use it to cook in.

Once you no longer hear bubbling in the pan, you know that the water is gone and that the coconut milk is almost pure fat. Then, add some chopped shallots; garlic; lemongrass; and galangal, which is a root that is similar to ginger but is a little deeper in flavor and woodier. Make sure that the galangal is sliced large enough so that you can see it; you don't want to eat it.

Because everything is cut up so small, you can add some pepper paste, called sambal oelek, almost immediately after adding the other ingredients. Remember that you can always add more, but you can't take any out, so be careful not to add too much because the dish will end up being too spicy.

Once the contents of the pan become aromatic, you can add chicken stock and coconut milk to the pan. In effect, you're making a cream soup. Add a little bit more chicken stock than coconut milk, but if you like it rich, use half chicken stock and half coconut milk. If you like it leaner, ease up on the coconut milk. Either way, the soup is going to be opaque and white.

While you are waiting for the liquid to come up to a boil, season it. Because you want to make the broth a little salty, add fish sauce as if it were salt. Whenever you use fish sauce, also add sugar to balance the intensity of the salt. Sugar also brings out a strong coconut flavor because coconut is sweet in its own right.

What Is Fish Sauce?

Fish sauce is made by letting small fish, such as anchovies, ferment for a few days and then putting them into a barrel—layering fish and salt until the barrel is full. Then, the barrel sits in the sun for about nine months. Afterward, the liquid that is found inside the barrel is fish sauce. This process began as a way to capture the protein in small fish that were readily available and abundant, but what was discovered was not just a fishiness, but also a savory flavor that is undeniable—like the savory flavor of soy sauce. It smells a little like bait, but when you know how to use it, it is a sauce that adds a lot of flavor to a dish.

As soon as the water is boiling, add chicken—cut up very small—to the pan. It's important that the liquid is boiling before the chicken goes in because protein is water soluble, so if you put it into cold liquid, the protein dissolves. Then, when the water comes up to a boil, the protein coagulates, and you will see scum

floating on the top of the water. If you put the protein into boiling liquid, then the protein sears, or seizes, on the outside, and the juices stay inside.

Once the chicken is in the pan, stir to break apart the pieces so that they don't stick together. Because the chicken was cut so small, by the time the liquid comes back to a boil, it's already cooked.

Next, add some vegetables, such as kaffir lime leaves, which are wild lime leaves. If you can't find them in the store, you can use a strip of lime zest. If you are using kaffir lime leaves, first remove the hard spine from each leaf. Think of it almost as if it were a bay leaf. Kaffir lime leaves lend a wonderful citrusy perfume to the broth.

Cooking with Lemongrass

When cooking with lemongrass, you only want to use the bottom eight inches—the part that's thick and juicy. You can either cut it into a big piece and then just bruise it with the back of your knife, thinking of it the way you might think of a bay leaf, or you can cut it up really small.

Then, add white button mushrooms sliced thin. Don't sauté them; just add them straight to the broth. Because they're sliced thin, they will cook quickly. Also add peeled, seeded, and diced tomatoes—or tomato concassé.

Once the broth comes back to a boil and the chicken is cooked, taste the soup. Squeeze in the juice of one lime to make the soup nice and bright. Finally, add just a little bit of cilantro and stir once more before taking the soup off the heat. With this soup, you want to avoid letting it simmer so long that the tomatoes begin to fall apart and it becomes a tomato soup. The soup only takes about five minutes to cook.

Gazpacho

To make the Spanish cold soup known as gazpacho, you are going to use a blender, which makes it easier than chopping all of the ingredients by hand. Start with some garlic, which can be mild and sweet or biting and hard, so start with half the amount that you think you will need. You can always add more, but you can't remove it once it has been added.

After adding the garlic to the blender, add some bread that has been soaked in water so that it is nice and soft. The bread will offer a body to the soup, and it

Shopping List

proportions to taste

garlic	ground black pepper
bread, soaked in water	water
green peppers	red wine vinegar
melon	olive oil (Spanish)
cucumber	lemon verbena
tomatoes	thyme
salt	

will bind excess liquid so that the soup won't look watery—instead, it will be a little creamy. Then, add green peppers, melon, cucumber, and tomatoes. The riper these items are, the better this soup will be.

Put the lid on the blender and blend the ingredients. The blender whips air into the mixture, so as it sits, the color will tend to darken. You're going to put it in the refrigerator, so the air will come out of the mixture anyway. After tasting

the blended mixture, season it with salt and pepper. If the consistency looks a little thick, add some water.

One way to think about this soup when you're seasoning it is to imagine it as a salad. Dress the salad—not just with salt and pepper, but also with oil and vinegar. Specifically, add some red wine vinegar and a good-quality olive oil. In fact, it would be great if you could use a Spanish olive oil, which tend to be milder than Tuscan olive oils. The tremendous amount of power that Tuscan olive oils have might overwhelm the vegetables. Don't be shy about being generous with the olive oil. A vinaigrette is three parts oil to one part vinegar, and that ratio applies to this mixture.

The downside to making soup in a blender is that you lose all of the texture of the vegetables, so leave some of the vegetables out of the blender. Dice them up very small and very carefully, and add them to the soup to give it some textural interest.

Ladle a portion of the soup into a bowl. If you have time, put the soup in the refrigerator for an hour or two. However, don't serve it ice cold. If you want to garnish it, save some of the vegetables and float them on the top of the soup. You can also add some fresh herbs, such as lemon verbena—which has a nice lemony flavor—thyme, and some pepper.

French Onion Soup

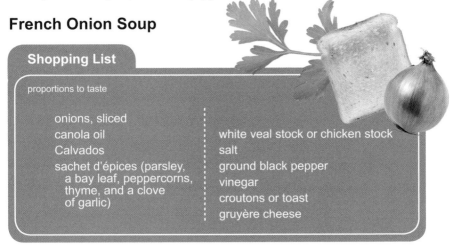

Shopping List

proportions to taste

onions, sliced
canola oil
Calvados
sachet d'épices (parsley,
    a bay leaf, peppercorns,
    thyme, and a clove
    of garlic)

white veal stock or chicken stock
salt
ground black pepper
vinegar
croutons or toast
gruyère cheese

To make french onion soup, which originated in Paris, start by slicing up about a quart or more of onions. It might look like a large pile of them to begin with, but when they cook, they will shrink. Sauté the onions in a fat that can withstand the heat of a pan over time. For this purpose, you have two options: clarified butter or canola oil. Clarified butter is just butter that has had the milk solids and buttermilk—which will burn easily—removed from it, and that

raises the smoke point of butter significantly. You could use either option, but in this case, canola oil is preferred.

Add the sliced onions to a very hot pan with oil as soon as the oil starts smoking. Stir them just to coat them with fat. Then, let them cook for about 35 minutes. Do not continually stir them because if you do, they might mat down, capturing the moisture underneath them, and with moisture, they can't brown properly.

Adding Salt and Pepper

Many people mistakenly think that if a little pepper is good, then a lot of pepper has to be better. However, too much pepper can quickly ruin a dish, so don't overdo it. Typically, you should use about six times as much salt as pepper.

Little by little, you will notice some color taking hold, and you want to flip the browned onions as one side browns. If you see the bottom of the pan beginning to burn—if you see the fond beginning to develop and if it looks darker than you think is appropriate—pull the pan off the heat and scrape it with your spoon or spatula so that any residual onion doesn't burn. A wooden spoon with a flat end is best for this task. If using a scraper of some kind doesn't work, add a little bit of liquid to deglaze the bottom and then let the liquid evaporate. Continue to cook the onions until you see a dark caramelized onion color—almost mahogany.

Once the onions are fully browned, the next step is to deglaze the pan. To do so, add some Calvados, or apple brandy, to the pan and use it to clean up everything that sticks to the bottom and sides of the pan. Bring the liquid up to a boil.

Make a sachet d'épices by gathering thyme, parsley, a bay leaf, peppercorns, and garlic in a small piece of cheesecloth. Tie it into what amounts to nothing more than a tea bag and add it to the pan.

Some recipes for onion soup call for white veal stock while others call for chicken stock. The veal stock offers gelatin and depth of flavor, and chicken stock offers freshness and aroma, so a blend of veal and chicken stock—in equal measure—is a great compromise. Add a little bit of broth to deepen the flavor and give it more texture. Then, reduce it, allowing the liquid in the pan to simmer for about 20 minutes.

After 20 minutes, you will notice that some of the color leaves the onions and is transferred to the broth. Scoop the sachet d'épices out of the pan and discard it. Taste the soup. Because of the sweetness of the onions, which can be overwhelming, add some salt and pepper. The salt will help balance the sweetness of the onions. If it is still too sweet after adding the salt, a splash of vinegar can cut through some of the sweetness.

When the broth is done cooking, you could simply ladle it into a soup bowl. Traditionally, however, the soup is served in a crock with a crust of bread (which could even be stale bread that has been toasted) on the top so that when cheese is added, it doesn't sink into the soup.

To make this soup in the traditional way, ladle the soup into a crock—almost all of the way full. Then, take some croutons or toast and put it on top. Then, float a piece of gruyère cheese (which has a wonderful savory flavor) on top of the bread, which holds the cheese aloft. Put the crock into the broiler that has been preheated. You want the cheese to begin to melt and then begin to brown. Ultimately, you want the cheese to be nice and bubbly.

Depending on the broiler you have, it might take as long as three minutes for the cheese to reach the brownness that is desired. If you wait too long before you put the crock into the broiler, the dried bread will begin to absorb all of the soup, and when the bread gets really wet, it will sink into the soup. Be careful with the bowl when you take it out of the broiler because it will be very hot.

Ribollita

Shopping List

proportions to taste

leftover soup
leftover bread
parmesan cheese
olive oil (Tuscan)

If you ever have leftover soup, you can make a Tuscan soup called ribollita, which means "recooked" or "reboiled." Minestrone soup, for example, is a thick, hearty soup that is loaded with greens, cabbage, beans, and vegetables and is a great soup to use for this purpose.

To make ribollita, bring your leftover soup up to a boil. If you have some leftover bread lying around, add it to the soup. When the soup comes up to a boil, the bread will become soaked with soup and tender, so you can break the bread into big chunks at that point.

After the soup has warmed and the bread has softened, put the soup into a bowl. Sprinkle some parmesan cheese on the top and then pour the best-quality Tuscan olive oil you can get on the top as well. Tuscan olive oil is a little pungent and bitter, but it is vegetal and makes the soup pop. Don't be shy about being generous with the olive oil. In fact, leave the oil on the table when you serve the soup so that people can help themselves.

From Fettuccine to Orecchiette— Fresh and Dry Pastas

Lesson 18

Human beings rely on wheat for nutrition, and pasta has sustained people since the dawn of agriculture. Every culture, it seems, has some sort of pasta. In Italy, there is an abundance of spaghetti. In Southeast Asia, you will find plenty of rice noodles. In Latin America, people consume large quantities of fideo, and in Northern Europe, people eat a dumpling called spaetzle. This lesson will teach you that while there are many varieties of dried pasta that you can buy at the store, you can also make fresh pasta from scratch, which is a fun activity that is also very rewarding.

Types of Pasta

There are many types of pasta. Rustic pastas include rigatoni, penne, shells, and fusilli. Delicate pastas include linguini; fettuccini; and angel hair, which is probably the most delicate.

Soup pastas can be captured on a spoon and eaten easily when you are eating a soup that contains pasta. When you are eating soup, you don't want something that is long and hangs off both ends of your spoon. Soup pastas are so small that they are great for use in pasta salads as well.

Whole wheat pasta is made from whole grain, which contains fiber and extra nutrition. However, whole wheat pasta has a very different flavor and maybe

even a more rustic texture than regular pasta, so you have to choose a sauce that is more assertive than usual. Nutritionally, pasta that is made with wheat flour and bean flour is a complete protein.

Fresh Fettuccini

Shopping List

proportions to taste

all-purpose flour
eggs
water

Because the only ingredients you need for making fresh pasta are all-purpose flour, eggs, and water, it is important to focus on the technique. You are going to be looking for a very specific texture when making fresh pasta. First, start the food processor and introduce some eggs, flour, and water. When you turn the food processor on, the ingredients won't form a large ball of dough; instead, the flour will moisten and look almost like wet sand cascading in on itself.

After the ingredients are mixed, dump the contents of the food processor onto a clean surface. Then, you can either knead the dough—so that it sticks together—on the surface or in a pasta machine, but it is easier to knead it in the machine by repeatedly rolling the dough and folding it.

Before kneading the dough, gather the ingredients and press them together. You don't want the dough to be really wet; otherwise, the pasta might stick to itself. The dough should hold together—albeit very loosely. The reason it should not stick together very tightly is that, at this point in the process, the flour hasn't been fully hydrated, and gluten hasn't begun to develop. Gluten is a protein in flour that, as it is manipulated with water, becomes more and more elastic, which is what makes pasta and bread what they are.

Once the dough is ready, roll it through a pasta machine. Typically, pasta machines can attach to your kitchen counter, and they often have a hand crank that is used to crank the pasta through the rollers. Most pasta machines also have gradations for the rollers, which can be chosen by turning a dial. Set the rollers as wide apart as they can go, and feed the dough through them. This will result in a pretty raggedy mass of dough. Then, gather the dough and press it together again. When you send the dough through the machine a second time, you will notice that the dough is less raggedy. Fold it in half and send it through the machine a third time, at which point you can start to see that the edges are no longer ragged because the gluten has begun to develop. You need a strong flour that has gluten in it if your pasta is going to have the appropriate texture.

Continue to roll and fold the dough until it is very smooth and developed. It will feel almost like a new baseball glove or a new pair of shoes; compare the dough to the feel of firm, smooth leather. As you roll the dough through the pasta machine, bring the rollers a little bit closer together than they were when you started. As the dough becomes firmer, it becomes difficult to put through the rollers after folding it in half, so roll it thinner before you fold it and then open the rollers up all the way.

Once the dough is smooth and developed, fold it together, put it in a ziplock bag so that it doesn't dry out, and set it aside to rest for about 20 to 30 minutes. If you were to continue to roll the dough instead of letting it rest, the gluten in the flour would become so tight that it would begin to tear, and the dough would be destroyed.

After the dough has rested, it should feel a little bit softer and moister than it was. It should not, however, be sticky; if it is sticky, then either you added too much liquid or didn't use enough flour. If you live in an area that is humid, your flour may be a little moister than it would be in dryer areas.

Put the dough back through the pasta machine, rolling it thinner and thinner. Each time you roll it through, bring the rollers closer together until the dough is the thickness of fettuccine—in this case. As the rollers are set closer and closer together, the dough will become longer and longer. If the dough becomes too long to be manageable, simply cut it into smaller pieces.

At some point, you have to decide when the pasta is thin enough—keeping in mind that as pasta cooks, it will swell and most likely double in size. The first

time you make pasta, pay attention to how thinly you roll it. Then, after you cook it, evaluate the finished product so that you can adjust the thinness for the next time.

Once the pasta is thin enough, you can cut it either by putting it through an attachment that is added to the pasta machine or by using a knife. If the dough is sticky, dust it with some flour so that it doesn't stick to itself. Then, put it through the cutting attachment on the pasta machine. Once the pasta is cut, put it onto a tray, such as a cookie sheet, and sprinkle some cornmeal on top to keep the noodles from sticking to each other.

As you roll the dough through the cutter, you want to cut it off after it is about 10 inches long, which is about how long dried pastas—such as spaghetti or fettuccine—are when you buy them in boxes.

After the pasta has been cut, it is ready to be dropped into boiling water. If you are not ready to cook it yet, the pasta can sit at room temperature, and as long as it is separated and not sticking, it will very quickly dry out to become dried pasta from fresh pasta. Even if you put it in the refrigerator in a plastic bag before cooking it as fresh pasta, it may start to stick to itself. Instead, if you make extra pasta, just let it dry and cook it as dried pasta later.

Pasta Carbonara

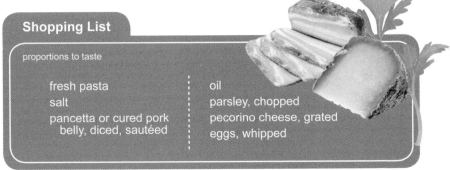

Shopping List

proportions to taste

fresh pasta	oil
salt	parsley, chopped
pancetta or cured pork belly, diced, sautéed	pecorino cheese, grated
	eggs, whipped

Pasta carbonara is pasta in the style of the coal miner. This is a simple dish that was probably once made for coal miners in Italy. Basically, this dish involves pasta, bacon, and eggs.

To make pasta carbonara with fresh pasta, bring a large pot of water to boil. You should use about six times as much water as pasta. Season the water with a lot of salt; you want it to taste a little like seawater. In other words, it should taste like a properly seasoned broth.

Once the water starts boiling, add the pasta to the pot and stir it so that it doesn't stick to itself. If you don't have a pot that comes with a colander that fits directly into it, you can drain the pasta into a colander over a bowl. Don't pour the starchy, seasoned water down the drain because you will use a little bit of it when you are almost finished cooking this dish.

When you add the pasta to the pot, the temperature of the water will drop, but once the water returns to a boil, cook the pasta for about two to four minutes, making sure to stir it occasionally. Fresh pasta cooks about twice as fast as dried pasta.

While the pasta is cooking, sauté some diced pancetta—or cured pork belly, which you can think of as bacon that has

When Is Pasta Done Cooking?

To determine whether pasta is done cooking, you can break it, and if the core is still white and chalky, then the flour has not cooked all the way to the center. You can also taste it to see whether it is done cooking. Many people say that pasta should be cooked "al dente," which means "to the tooth." In other words, it should not be chewy or overcooked, but it should have enough texture to retain its form on a plate.

not been smoked—in a pan with oil until it is golden. On the bottom of the pan, the fond, or the drippings from the pork, will form. Make sure that you don't burn it. The pancetta fat will also be in the pan; you want to keep that, so don't pour it out.

If you taste the pancetta, you will find that it is a little bit salty, which is what you would expect from bacon, so make sure that you take that into account when you add any final seasoning to this dish. Once the pancetta is browned, remove it from the pan, leaving the fond on the bottom for a short time.

While you are waiting for the pasta to finish cooking, chop some parsley. Too often, people consider parsley to be just a garnish—something green to sprinkle on top—but it is also a vegetable, and it's actually a pretty tasty vegetable. It lends freshness, vitality, and green grassiness to this dish. While waiting, you can also grate some pecorino cheese, which is a sharp cheese. In addition, you can whip some eggs in preparation for when you add them to this dish later.

Check on the pasta. When it is done cooking, remove the pot from the heat and drain it of all the excess liquid. Remember to turn your stove's burner off. Once the pasta is drained, put the pasta into a pan. Then, add some of the pasta water to the heated pan that held the pancetta to recapture the flavor of the pancetta, scraping up the fond and dissolving it as it cooks.

While the pasta is hot, toss it with the pancetta, fat, and fond from the pan. Then, add the chopped parsley and the eggs. You have to be careful once you add the eggs because you want to keep the mixture moving by stirring constantly. Ultimately, the eggs will still be a little bit soft. It won't take very long because the pasta is hot. Finally, mix in some pecorino cheese. When you are ready to serve this pasta, add a little bit extra cheese on top of the dish.

Angel Hair Pasta with Light Sauce

Shopping List

proportions to taste

angel hair pasta	parsley, coarsely chopped
onions	basil chiffonade
olive oil	cheese, shaved
garlic	ground black pepper
tomatoes, cut	pasta water
	salt

For this dish, instead of using fresh pasta, you can use dry pasta—specifically, angel hair pasta, which is probably the most delicate pasta. Because angel hair pasta is so delicate, it is best served with a light sauce because a heavy sauce would overwhelm the pasta.

When you are ready to boil the angel hair pasta in water, don't add oil to the water to prevent the pasta from sticking together because although the pasta won't stick together, the sauce won't stick to the pasta either. Simply add the pasta to a pot of boiling water and it will be done cooking in about two minutes.

While the pasta is cooking, make the light sauce. Start by adding onions to a hot pan with olive oil and sweat them until they are translucent. Add garlic to the pan as well and cook it just until it becomes aromatic. Then, add some tomatoes that have been left chunky so that they don't fall apart too much. Finally, add some coarsely chopped parsley and basil chiffonade to the pan. Basil will turn black if you just chop it up and add it to the pan, so use the chiffonade technique to roll it up and cut it into ribbons.

Prepare for plating by shaving some cheese with a vegetable peeler. It is very common to add grated cheese to pasta, but the cheese may melt and clump the hot pasta together, so shaving it in larger pieces with a vegetable peeler may help keep the pasta strands separated.

When the pasta is done cooking, drain it. Then, turn up the heat of the pan and add the pasta to the pan. Then, add pepper and mix all of the ingredients in the pan together. Don't add salt too early in the process of cooking this dish.

If the pasta starts sticking to the pan, you can add some good-quality olive oil, which will also add a bit more flavor. As an alternative to the oil, you can add some pasta water, which will also add flavor and loosen the mixture. Taste the pasta with the sauce, adding salt and pepper as needed. Then, add the shaved cheese. When you are ready to serve the pasta, put it in a bowl and add some olive oil, pepper, and a few more pieces of cheese on top.

Orecchiette and Broccoli Rabe

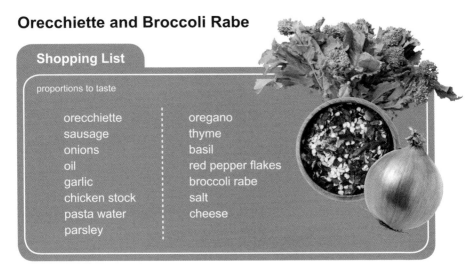

Shopping List

proportions to taste

orecchiette	oregano
sausage	thyme
onions	basil
oil	red pepper flakes
garlic	broccoli rabe
chicken stock	salt
pasta water	cheese
parsley	

While angel hair pasta is very delicate, orecchiette is a hearty and rustic pasta that is named after pigs' ears. Because orecchiette is on the tougher and thicker end of the pasta spectrum, it takes about 11 to 12 minutes to cook. Because it is tough and thick, however, it can stand up to big flavors, such as those found in tomatoes and sausages.

To make this dish, start by adding the orecchiette to a pot of boiling water. While the pasta is cooking, add some sausage and onions to a hot pan with oil and allow them to brown, which will take about 15 minutes. Then, add garlic to the pan. In a rustic dish like this, it is okay to cut the garlic into large pieces.

As the contents of the pan come up to simmer, you might notice that the pan becomes pretty dry, so have some chicken stock on hand to loosen the mixture up and to flavor it. If the sauce still seems to need some liquid after adding the chicken stock, you can amend it with some pasta water.

Allow the sauce to simmer until it looks like a bolognese sauce. Then, add some parsley, oregano, thyme, and basil. Because this is a rustic sauce, you can add these herbs in large chunks. You can also add pepper flakes if you want the sauce to be spicy.

When the sauce seems to be almost ready, add some broccoli rabe to the pan. Broccoli rabe is bitter, and you don't want it to lose its bitterness in the cooking process, so cut it into bite-sized pieces. Add it to the pan warm so that when the pasta comes out of the water, the dish will be ready to be served.

When you think the pasta is done cooking, evaluate its consistency by tasting a piece of it. Pasta is thirsty, and the starch in the pasta will absorb moisture, so it will taste better if it is stirred in with the contents of the pan and cooked briefly.

Once the pasta is added to the sauce, evaluate the flavor of the pasta. Specifically, evaluate the dish's saltiness and add salt if needed. In this dish, the sausage should taste more like a complement to the pasta and broccoli rabe than a big flavor on its own. Finally, add cheese to the dish. You can always add pasta water to this dish if it is too dry.

When you plate a portion of this pasta, add a little bit of cheese on top. If you have leftovers of this dish, put it in a gratin dish and add oil and some pasta water so that it is on the loose side. You could easily build another meal out of this pasta by layering some cheese and the pasta in a dish. Then, put it in the oven at 350 degrees for about 30 minutes.

Meat—From Spatchcocked Chicken to Brined Pork Chops
Lesson 19

While you have learned plenty of techniques involving meat, in this lesson, you are going to look at meat as an ingredient. You probably have strategies for buying meat. You might spend as much money as you can afford to get the best meat possible, or you might just look for the bargains. The appropriate decisions regarding when to spend and when to save on the price of meat probably lie tangled between those two extremes. This lesson will hopefully make you a more informed consumer.

Spatchcocked Chicken

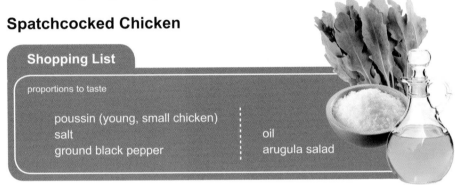

Shopping List

proportions to taste

poussin (young, small chicken)
salt
ground black pepper

oil
arugula salad

In general, an older animal has more flavor and fat than a younger animal. A young, small chicken—called a poussin—has a mild flavor, so you should cook it so that it gets a lot of browning, season it assertively, and serve it with a salad that has a lot of flavor.

Instead of roasting a chicken for an hour and a half, a technique called spatchcocking is a way that you can roast a chicken very quickly. Start by cutting the spine out of the bird by cutting on either side of the neck with a pair of poultry shears. Once you open the bird up, cut the cartilage closest to the wings and then pull out the keel bone, or breastbone. With the breastbone out, the chicken lays flat. Trim the wings off as well. Because you are going to roast the chicken flat in a pan, it should cook very quickly.

Place a pan on the stove on high heat. Season the chicken with salt and pepper on both sides and rub some oil into the chicken as well. Also, preheat the oven at 475 to 500 degrees.

Once you start to see a little bit of smoke coming off of the oil, that means that the oil is as hot as it can be without it breaking down. Put the chicken in the

pan with its skin side down, and you will hear it sizzle. Let the chicken cook for a few minutes.

You can even put a brick (covered with foil and preheated in the oven for a while at 475 degrees) on top of the chicken to hold the skin in close contact with the pan below so that the skin becomes golden and crispy. Then, put the chicken in the preheated oven for about 20 minutes. Remove the brick to determine whether the chicken is fully cooked. When it is fully cooked, separate it into portions and serve it with an arugula salad.

Brined Pork Chops

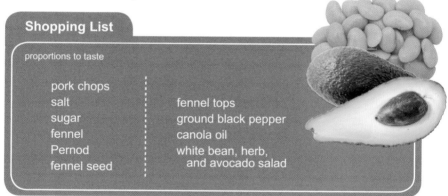

Shopping List

proportions to taste

pork chops
salt
sugar
fennel
Pernod
fennel seed

fennel tops
ground black pepper
canola oil
white bean, herb,
   and avocado salad

Pork is the other white meat. Since about the 1980s, pork has been bred to be leaner and leaner so that it can compete with chicken breast. Pork is a fairly lean cut of meat, but that can be a problem in the kitchen because when you cook a very lean meat, it can dry out unless you are really careful.

Pork is not graded the way beef is graded—prime or choice, for example—so consumers have no way of understanding quality when it comes to pork. In the absence of a grading system, heritage pork has recently become the indicator

Meat-Cooking Tip

When meat first hits a pan, if the meat is a little wet, it will stick to the pan, but as it begins to dry out, it will free itself, so don't fuss with it too soon.

of quality. Heritage pork grows more slowly and likely puts on more fat, and it's entirely possible that it tastes better, but it also costs a lot more.

A brine is nothing more than a salty liquid that meat is soaked in. It can be flavored with a number of different things. To make a brine, put a pot of water on the stove. Add salt and balance the saltiness with some sugar. Then, add fennel, Pernod (which has the flavor of fennel in it), fennel seed, and fennel tops. Once the water comes up to a boil, remove it from the heat and cool it down. When it's cold, it's ready to accept the meat that you want to brine.

A thick two- or three-inch pork chop may take two full days to absorb the salt. Over that span of time, with more salt on the outside and less salt on the inside of the meat, the salty water will start to flow into the cells of the meat, causing it to become plumped. The meat will gain about 10 percent in weight. This also means that the seasoning will enter the meat, resulting in more flavor. In addition, the salt will inhibit the protein from clenching up as tightly when it cooks, so you will be left with a piece of meat that is more tender. Because the meat will soak up the extra moisture in the pot, it will also be juicier. Finally, the meat—even before you cook it—will last longer because the salty environment inhibits bacteria from growing.

Start with one-inch pork chops that have been brined in the refrigerator for 24 hours. After you take them out of the brine, blot them dry. You don't have to add salt to the pork because it absorbed plenty of salt from the brine, but you

can still add some pepper. When you cook the pork, be aware that there is sugar in the brine, and sugar likes to caramelize, so you have to regulate the heat carefully.

Start cooking the brined pork on the stove by adding some canola oil to a heated pan. Once the pan starts to smoke, sauté the pork on one side and then flip it over. As soon as the meat is in the pan, turn the heat down just a little bit because of the sugar. Once the meat is browned, put the whole pan in the oven, which should be set at about 450 degrees. At an inch thick, the pork should take about eight minutes to cook. Cook the pork until its internal temperature reaches about 145 degrees; at that temperature, you can expect a little bit of pinkness inside of it. When the pork is fully cooked, slice it and serve it with some white beans mixed with herbs and a little bit of avocado.

Grading Meat

Grading is a way of understanding quality in meat, which, for the most part, has to do with how much intramuscular fat that the meat contains. A steak that has a grading of prime has a lot of fat that makes its way through the muscle. One step below a grade of prime is choice. Below choice is select, which doesn't have nearly the amount of intramuscular fat that a prime steak has. Below select are cutter and canner, which you don't often see on the market. Certified Angus Beef is not a grade; it is actually a brand. It is guaranteed to be the top 20 percent of choice.

Grading of meat is not mandatory; instead, it is a voluntary practice that costs money. Therefore, when packers choose to grade meat, they typically do it so that consumers know what they are buying.

Roasted Prime Rib

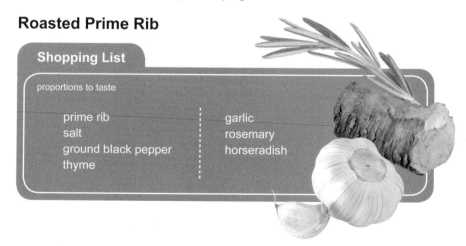

Shopping List

proportions to taste

prime rib
salt
ground black pepper
thyme

garlic
rosemary
horseradish

A prime rib of beef is probably the most expensive piece of meat you will ever buy. Prime rib is not necessarily prime meat. You can find a graded prime rib, but it is still called "prime" rib as a matter of course.

A prime rib is the rib of the animal, which is the part of the animal that doesn't get a lot of exercise, so it's very tender. To cook prime rib, start by cutting the meat off of the rib bones. Then, tie the meat back onto the rib bones, which will act like little racks and will also lend flavor to the meat. To do this, wind one string lengthwise over the meat so that the bone stays tight to the meat while it's cooking. A butcher can also do this for you.

After you tie the meat to the bones but before you put the meat into the oven, season the meat pretty assertively with salt and add a little bit of pepper. You can also add thyme, garlic, and/or rosemary if you want to. Then, put the meat into a roasting pan and into an oven that is heated to a relatively high temperature. Then, turn the temperature down and roast the meat at about 350 degrees for about an hour and a half to an hour and three quarters. Once the meat reaches an internal temperature of 125 degrees, it should be browned and should come out of the oven.

Taking the Temperature of Meat

When you take the temperature of a piece of meat, make sure that the probe does not hit a bone because the bones carry the heat of the oven into the meat much more effectively. Likewise, make sure that the probe is not buried in a big piece of fat but, instead, in the thickest part or in the center of the meat.

Once you take the meat out of the oven, let it rest for about half an hour. Initially, the heat that is inherent in the meat will have to dissipate. Some of it will pass off into the cool of the room, and some of it will carry on to the center of the meat and give it an extra 10 degrees of cooking. If you don't let the meat rest, some of the juices will flow out of the meat, and it will become less moist and juicy.

After about half an hour of letting it rest, transfer the meat over to a cutting board. Then, take all of the strings off that you had tied on the meat before cooking it. The bones should separate very easily from the meat. Finally, slice the meat. If you like your meat well-done, take your portion from the end cut. As you make your way to the middle, the meat will become progressively more rare.

Serve the prime rib with horseradish. There should be plenty of pan juices to make a gravy, which is thickened with flour, or au jus, which is not thickened with flour. If you choose to serve the prime rib with horseradish, make sure to save the juices from the meat, which you can use in a soup at some point in the future.

Blue Cheese Burgers

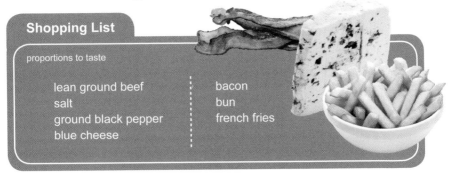

Shopping List

proportions to taste

lean ground beef	bacon
salt	bun
ground black pepper	french fries
blue cheese	

To make burgers, start with some lean ground beef that is about 20 percent fat and 80 percent lean. Meat that is used for burgers needs to have the right amount of fat—not too much and not too little. If the meat contains too much fat, it will all bleed out, and without any fat, or very little fat, your burger will taste dry. In addition, buy good-quality meat, and if you can get it freshly ground, that is even better.

Be aware that ground beef can be hazardous if you don't keep it refrigerated right up until you need it. Bacteria is a surface phenomenon on a piece of meat that is not a problem when the surface of the meat is cooked, but if you grind all of the meat together, then you mix the bacteria throughout the meat, and it can be problematic.

Start by shaping the ground beef, making each burger a little convex so that each has a little hollow on the top. The meat will begin to contract when you start to cook it, and when it does, it might bunch up in the center and turn into a meatball unless you begin with it slightly indented. Don't overmanipulate the meat, and don't pack it too tightly. Once you have shaped the ground beef, season the burgers with some salt and pepper. Don't season them too early because salt can dry meat out over time. Then, cook the burgers in a cast-iron pan on the stove or on a grill.

While the burgers are cooking, don't take your spatula and press on them really hard because that squeezes the juices out of the meat. When you are cooking burgers, there's a chance that the burger meat will stick to the pan or grill. As it cooks, the meat begins to shrink up, and it typically frees itself, so don't move it around too early in the cooking process. After a few minutes, flip each burger and turn the heat up just a little bit.

One of the best things about burgers is that many toppings and condiments are readily available to you. Some common toppings and condiments include various types of cheeses, bacon, sautéed mushrooms, fried eggs, tomatoes, lettuce, mustard, mayonnaise, ketchup, barbecue sauce, and even chutney. A great combination of condiments is blue cheese and bacon. You can put the bacon into the pan with the burger and let it warm up; then, crumble some blue cheese on top and let it melt.

When the burger is done cooking, slide it onto a bun. Because the bun of a burger is basically two-thirds of the dish, spend some extra money on a good-quality burger bun. Then, build your burger with whatever condiments you desire and add some french fries on the side.

Seafood—From Market to Plate

Lesson 20

Seafood is one of the last wild crops. It is pulled from a dark and watery world and seems somehow unfamiliar and a little bit challenging. Even if you have never eaten seafood, you probably know that it is good for you and think that you should be eating more of it. Many people have eaten seafood that is expensive but, quite frankly, tastes fishy. This lesson will help you understand what to look for when buying seafood.

Buying Seafood

The first rule of buying seafood is to stay flexible. When fishermen or fisherwomen go out to fish, what they bring back is really shaped by fate and a little bit of their skill. Try to establish a relationship with a fishmonger by getting to know him or her, telling him or her what you like and don't like, and taking his or her recommendations. You can also take advantage of the services that he or she might offer, such as filleting or gutting a fish. It is worth paying for a skilled person to scale a fish and cut it into portions for you.

To analyze the quality of a fish, the first thing that you should do is feel the outside of the fish. If it's slimy, that shouldn't be a problem because it's that slime that protects the fish and helps it slide through the water when it's alive. If it feels slimy but also smells bad, that's a very different kind of slime, and that's a problem. When assessing aroma, you will first start to notice aroma probably in the belly, so open the belly and give it a sniff.

The flesh of the fish should be firm; it should spring back when you press it. If you press it and a small indentation lingers, that is a sign that it's an older fish. In addition, the scales should be firmly attached. If you rub the fish from the tail to the head and the scales come off, chances are that it is an older fish. Furthermore, if the fins are dried out, broken, and cracked, it could be indicative of a fish that has been mishandled or been out of the water for too long. The fins should be moist and full.

The gills of the fish are where it breathes. Over time, the gills will go from a deep reddish or pink color to sort of a deep brick red or even brown, and as they progress from red and pink to brown, you know that the fish is getting older. It is not uncommon that the gills will be taken out of a fish because they will spoil more quickly, but if the gills are missing, then you should look at other indicators of quality to determine the age of the fish.

Make sure to examine the eye of the fish because eyes age as well. Once the fish is dead and out of the water, its eyes become a little bit cloudy, so a clear eye is indicative of a fish that is fresh. When you look at a really fresh fish on your cutting board, it should look vital. An older fish does not look vital.

If you're buying fillets of fish instead of a whole fish, the fillets should be vital and not discolored. They should look fresh and moist, and the flesh should not be torn. The fillets should be firm and should smell fresh and briny.

Freshness of Fish

Fish live in salted water that is possibly even colder than a refrigerator, so the enzymes and bacteria that are inherent in fish have learned how to work at cold temperatures. When you take a fish out of that cold environment and put it into a refrigerator, the bacteria start to grow very quickly and the enzymes begin to break the flesh down, so you need to keep fish really cold to prevent that from happening. The easiest way to do that is to keep the fish on ice.

When you go shopping for fish, make sure to buy your fish at the end of your trip, and if you can take a little cooler with you, that's even better. As a rule of thumb, every hour that a fish spends at room temperature shortens its shelf life by an entire day.

Ceviche

Shopping List

proportions to taste

fresh fish, cut
lime juice
salt
onion, diced
tomato, diced
serrano peppers, diced small
picholine olives

cilantro
avocado
tomato juice
dried Mexican oregano
sugar
fried tortilla chips

The best thing to do with fresh fish is to make ceviche. With ceviche, freshness counts, so make sure that you evaluate your fish for freshness before deciding to make ceviche with it. To make ceviche, you need to cook the fish in acidity—namely, lime juice. The fish will turn opaque as soon as it gets mixed with the lime juice, and then over the following 10 minutes, the opaqueness will spread toward the center of the fish.

With a sharp knife, start by cutting the fish into thin pieces—probably a little bit less than a quarter of an inch thick—and once you have cut all the slices, line them up and cut them across. Then, pour lime juice over the fish and briefly stir it. Season it with a little bit of salt and let it soak in the lime juice for about 10 minutes.

Then, prepare the rest of the ceviche. Depending on the flavor profile you're looking for, you might find a recipe that uses ingredients that are fairly simple, but if you want a full-flavored ceviche, start by adding some diced onion and tomato to a bowl. Then, add some serrano peppers, which can be very hot, so make sure you dice them up very small. Don't add too much until you're sure that you can tolerate the heat. Then, stir in some picholine olives, which are briny green olives. Add some cilantro for its bright, citrusy flavor and some avocado for its richness. Moisten the mixture with tomato juice.

Season the mixture with some dried Mexican oregano, which is reminiscent of fresh marjoram. Make sure to properly season it with salt, and then dress it with a little bit of lime.

After about 10 minutes, drain the fish from the lime juice and fish water that has dripped off of the fish. Gently stir the fish and garniture together so that the avocado doesn't break up, and then taste the completed dish. You might find that adding a few pinches of sugar can take the edge off the harsh lime. Serve the ceviche on a plate with some fried tortilla chips. If you want it to look fancy, you can serve the ceviche in a small martini glass.

Whole Roasted Fish with Fennel, Lemon, and Olive Oil

Shopping List

proportions to taste

striped bass, whole	white wine
Florence fennel	bay leaves
olive oil	thyme
onions, chopped	lemon, sliced
salt	ground black pepper
garlic	parsley
tomato, diced	fennel tops

This dish involves roasting a whole fish—specifically, a striped bass—on a bed of Florence fennel. The reason to roast a fish whole is that when you cook meat on the bone, it absorbs the flavor from those bones and is much more flavorful and moister as a result.

To begin, slice some fennel. To a hot pan that has olive oil in it, add some chopped onions. Don't focus on browning the onions; instead, make sure that they become tender. Cook the onions until they begin to become translucent, adding a little bit of salt to help draw some of the moisture out. Then, add the fennel, which has a delicate anise flavor. Cook the fennel until it starts to soften a little bit, at which point you can add some garlic to the pan because you don't want the garlic to burn. Also add some diced tomato, white wine, a bay leaf, and a few branches of thyme. This is the base that the fish is going to cook on.

Before you cook it, the fish needs to be scaled. You should probably have a professional do this for you, but if you have a fish that has the scales on it, drag a knife—or even the edge of a kitchen spoon—backward against the way that the scales lay on the fish (from the tail toward the head). Little by little, the scales will pop off, but it can be a little messy, so keep a garbage bag nearby. If you take your hand and run it along the fish, you will feel any scales that are still intact. You also need to cut all of the fins off because they tend to burn in a hot oven.

When you are roasting a fish in an oven at about 450 degrees, it will cook for about eight minutes per inch of thickness. Make sure to evaluate the fish at its thickest part before it goes into the oven. Season it on both sides with salt and pepper. Then, stuff the interior of the fish with branches of thyme, a few slices

of lemon, and a few bay leaves, which will all flavor the fish from the inside out as it cooks.

When you are ready to put the fish in the oven, make sure that you use a pan that is big enough to accommodate the fish. Then, put a little bit of oil in the bottom so that nothing sticks together and then add the bed of vegetables and lay the fish on top. The bed of vegetables will keep the fish moist and temper the heat of the oven, but the fish will still brown a little on the top. To facilitate that browning, top the fish with a little bit of good olive oil.

After about 15 to 20 minutes, depending on the thickness of the fish, you can pull it out of the oven. Take the fish off of its bed of vegetables, being careful with it because it is tender, and move it to a cutting board so that you can start to take the bones out of the fish. You should notice that the tail has become crispy, so trim it off. Every place where there was a fin, there will remain a small remnant of where the fin was attached, and you can pull out the bones that would have passed from the fin into the fish. To take the head off of the fish, use a knife to cut through the skin at the tail and continue cutting in a line down the center of the fish to separate the fish from its carcass. It should pull away, so if it is difficult, then it means that the fish is probably undercooked, and you should put it back in the oven.

Evaluating Doneness

When it comes to fish, you can evaluate doneness a number of different ways. You can poke it where it is the thickest, which is right behind the collar, or where the gill opening is. If you use a knife to make a cut in that area, you can expect the meat to be opaque all the way through. The meat should also separate easily from the bone.

After you have taken the bones out of the fish, you can remove the thyme, lemon, and bay leaves from the body. Then, put the vegetables that cooked with the fish on a plate and carefully move the fish back on top of the vegetables. You can garnish this dish with parsley, or even some fennel tops, and a few slices of lemon. This dish can be paired with a glass of sauvignon blanc.

Mussels with White Wine and Shallots

In the case of mollusks—whether you are dealing with clams, mussels, or oysters—you have to handle them a little bit differently than you would handle fish. If you were to bury live mollusks in ice to keep them fresh, they would likely freeze to death, so don't ice them. Instead, keep them in the refrigerator, covered with a damp towel. If you want to include some ice on the top of the towel, you can.

When you're buying mussels, you want them to be very heavy for their size, which means that there is still a lot of moisture in them. Also look for shells that are clean and tightly closed. If you come across a mussel that has its shell gapped open, that could mean that the mussel is dead. If you squeeze the shell and it closes, then it's still alive, but if it doesn't close, that means that it is dead.

Types of Mussels

PEI mussels are good-quality mussels that come from Prince Edward Island, and there are times of the year when PEI mussels are not available, so there's another variety that you can find called Mediterranean mussels, which are typically a little bit larger.

Mussels typically grow in a farm setting on ropes that hang downward, and they attach themselves to those ropes with a little beard, or a little piece of thread that sticks out. You can pull the beard off or cut it off, but if you pull it off, the mussel will die soon, so don't take the beard off until you are ready to serve the mussel. When you are ready to remove the beard, you can use a knife to grab it and pull it off.

To make this dish, start by putting some cut shallots into a pan with butter. You want to sweat the shallots until they are translucent, and if you cut them small, it won't take very long. Then, add some chopped thyme and white wine to the pan and bring it up to a boil. The goal is to steam the mussels open, which should only take about two to three minutes. During that time, the wine will mingle with the juices that come out of the mussels to create a full-flavored, savory liquid. As the liquid comes up to a boil, add the mussels to the pan and put a lid on it.

Periodically, you can shake the pan a little bit. It's a good sign if you see steam coming from the edge of the pan. When a mussel is cooked, it will open its shell. If a mussel's shell doesn't open, either it hasn't cooked long enough or it is dead but for some reason the shell is trapped shut. Once all of the shells have opened, transfer the mussels to a bowl.

Put the pan that contains the leftover liquid back on the heat for a short time. Taste the liquid, adding salt, pepper, and parsley as necessary. Then, add a few pieces of butter to the pan and stir the butter into the juices so that the liquid emulsifies. The butter will melt to make a creamy sauce. You could also add some garlic, some fennel seeds, and maybe even some Pernod. In addition, instead of finishing the sauce with butter, you could use cream.

Once the sauce is done cooking, pour it on top of the mussels. Serve this dish with some bread so that you can sop up the juices. You can also serve these mussels with french fries.

Vegetables in Glorious Variety

Lesson 21

The glorious variety of vegetables—which changes with every change of season—is what keeps food interesting. The category of vegetables includes seeds, such as corn, beans, and peas; pods, such as green beans; flowers, such as cauliflower and artichoke; roots, such as beets, parsnips, carrots, and turnips; bulbs, such as onions, shallots, and garlic; tubers, such as potatoes and sweet potatoes; and leaves, such as spinach, parsley, and cilantro. Every restaurant has the same meats to offer, but different assortments of vegetables bring interesting heterogeneity to the table.

Curried Roasted Cauliflower

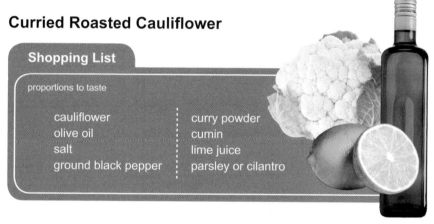

Shopping List

proportions to taste

cauliflower	curry powder
olive oil	cumin
salt	lime juice
ground black pepper	parsley or cilantro

To roast a cauliflower in the oven, start by cutting the core out of a head of cauliflower, making sure that your knife doesn't slip while doing so. Then, break it apart into florets. Keep the florets on the large size because larger pieces are easier to roast. You can even cut through the stem on some of them and then roughly break the halves apart. Move the cauliflower to a bowl, seasoning it first with olive oil and then with salt, a little bit of pepper, curry powder, and a little bit of cumin. Then, toss it all together.

Put the cauliflower on a sheet pan, or cookie sheet, and spread it out so that it roasts evenly. Then, put the pan into the oven at 400 to 450 degrees for about 20 minutes. If you check on it after 10 minutes, you should see a little bit of browning beginning to develop. When you check on it, you might want to stir it so that the oil that's on the pan coats the cauliflower. The cauliflower should be tender—not crunchy or hard. To evaluate it, poke the stem with a knife, which should go in easily, but the cauliflower should fall off the knife just as easily. It should also be browned along the edges.

When cauliflower is roasted, its flavor becomes concentrated. Some of the sweetness that's in the vegetable will become even sweeter, and that sweetness—side by side with the aromatic spices of curry—is delicious. In addition, when the cauliflower browns, it picks up a hint of bitterness, which is a nice contrast to the sweetness of the vegetable and the aromatic quality of the spices.

Roasted cauliflower tastes every bit as good at room temperature as it does hot out of the oven. Because there is so much flavor in it already, before you are ready to serve it, simply squeeze a lime over it and sprinkle some parsley or cilantro on top.

Baba Ghanoush

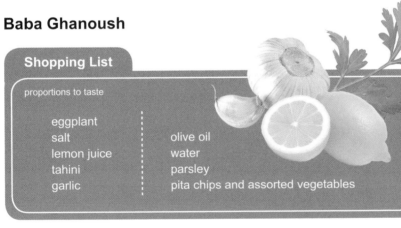

Shopping List

proportions to taste

eggplant	
salt	olive oil
lemon juice	water
tahini	parsley
garlic	pita chips and assorted vegetables

To make this rustic dish, start by roasting a whole eggplant on an open flame of a grill, making sure to turn the vegetable when necessary. It will become charred on the outside, and you eventually want the flesh to collapse completely. If don't want to roast over an open flame and don't like smoky flavors, you can also cut the eggplant in half, oil it, put it on a sheet pan, and place it in the oven until it has roasted, browned, and completely collapsed. It's imperative that it doesn't have any uncooked portions because it will taste bitter.

After the eggplant has been fully roasted and has cooled off a little, use a knife to help you carefully push the charred skin away from the eggplant. It's okay to leave a few pieces of dark skin on it because a little bit of charred skin actually enhances the nature of this dish. It makes it feel somehow more authentic because you know that it has been roasted over an open flame.

Transfer the eggplant to a bowl, where you can mash it with a fork if it is tender enough. You can transfer some of the smoky juices that collected in the pan as well. Add some salt right away so that it begins to dissolve, and then squeeze some lemon juice on top, using about a teaspoon of lemon juice per eggplant. As the eggplant sits, it can sometimes turn a little bit dark, and the lemon juice will help keep the color bright.

Next, add tahini, which is made of sesame seeds that have been ground to a paste—much like peanut butter. When you stir the tahini in, you will notice that the mixture will begin to tighten up. In addition to tahini, add some garlic, which is easy to add but almost impossible to remove, so don't add too much in the beginning. Then, emulsify the sauce with some olive oil, stirring as you add it drop by drop. The olive oil will make this mixture richer and give it a bright vegetable flavor. If it starts to look oily, then don't add it as quickly and make sure that you mix it so that the mixture can become creamy.

Taste this mixture—which would be considered a salad in the Middle East or in the eastern Mediterranean—and add more olive oil and lemon juice as needed. Finally, add a little bit of water to thin it out. Think of it as a dip that you can dip pita chips and vegetables in. You can also use it as a spread on sandwiches. Traditionally, baba ghanoush is spread out on a plate and topped with a little bit of oil and parsley.

The Color of Vegetables

Green beans get their color from chlorophyll, which hates acidity. When acidity is added to green beans, they turn a drab olive color. Green beans also don't like to be cooked for long amounts of time; instead, they like to cook quickly. Therefore, when cooking green beans, cook them in a large pot of boiling, salted water so that no matter how many beans you put in, the water doesn't stop boiling. An abundant amount of water will dilute any acidity that's inherent in the beans. Don't put a lid on it because the lid will just trap the acidity in. The acidity is volatile, but it will leave the pot with the steam. As soon as green beans are cooked, take them out of the pot and serve them quickly. Alternately, you can take them out of the pot and then shock them in ice water to stop the cooking. Then, you can reheat them when you want to use them later.

Boiled and Glazed Beets

Shopping List

proportions to taste

beets	chicken stock
salt	vinegar
cider vinegar	sugar
orange juice	butter
lemon juice	lime juice

Beets are red because of a pigment called anthocyanin, and while chlorophyll hates acidity, anthocyanin absolutely loves it. The red color of beets will turn vivid and bright in the presence of acid. The problem is that the pigment in beets is soluble in water, so if you peel a beet and put it in water, all of the color washes away. Therefore, you need to leave the peel, root, and stalk on when you boil them so that the color stays inside until after it has been cooked when you are ready to peel it.

In addition to red beets, golden beets like acidity as well. The color of golden beets is not as pronounced as it is for red beets, but golden beets will still become a little bit brighter in the presence of acidity.

To boil beets, start by putting them into a pot of water. Add salt to the water and then add some cider vinegar. Cook them until they are tender. Ultimately, when you pierce a beet with a knife, you want the knife to go in easily but, more importantly, come out easily. Therefore, if the beet clings to the knife, it is not done cooking.

As soon as the beets are cooked and are still hot from cooking, rub off the skin with a towel that you don't care much about. The skin should come off very easily, but this process will stain the towel. You can also rub off the root and even the top, which has stalks. If you encounter an area of skin that does not come off easily, you can use a knife to scrape that portion of skin off.

Beet Greens

If you buy beets that have the greens still attached, they need to be removed before you cook them, but you should consider keeping them and using them the same way you might use Swiss chard or escarole. You could add them to pasta or to a pot of minestrone. There's a lot of nutrition and flavor in beet greens.

The flavor of cooked beets is full, and they taste earthy in a way that people aren't used to, so make sure that the flavor of your seasoning is as aggressive as the flavor of the beets by making a glaze that contains orange juice, lemon juice, chicken stock, and vinegar. Also add some sugar, which will dissolve almost immediately when you stir everything together. Then, bring this mixture up to a boil and cook it until all of the liquid is gone. After about 20 minutes, it will turn into a thick, syrupy glaze. If you taste the glaze, it should have a sweet and sour flavor. After tasting it, you might want to add some salt. With the heat on high, introduce the beets to the glaze along with a little bit of butter. The glaze should coat the beets so that they glisten.

As the beets cook in the glaze, make sure to not reduce the liquid down so much that the water cooks out of it completely and the butter turns greasy and unpleasant. Once the beets are done cooking, you can remove them from the pan and add a splash of lime juice, which adds freshness, vitality, and acidity to the beets.

Carrot Osso Buco

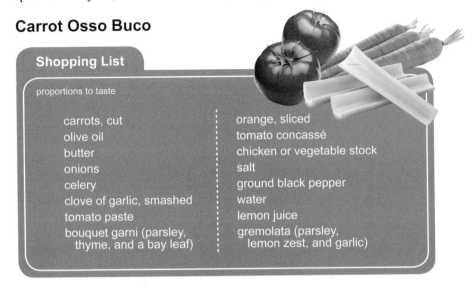

Shopping List

proportions to taste

carrots, cut	orange, sliced
olive oil	tomato concassé
butter	chicken or vegetable stock
onions	salt
celery	ground black pepper
clove of garlic, smashed	water
tomato paste	lemon juice
bouquet garni (parsley, thyme, and a bay leaf)	gremolata (parsley, lemon zest, and garlic)

Carrots may be the most forgiving of all of the vegetables. The pigment that gives carrots their color is not affected by whether something acidic is added to them or whether they are cooked for a long or short amount of time.

Osso buco is a dish that is usually reserved for veal shanks. The name means "bone with a hole in it." Because carrots are just as tough as veal shanks, you can cook them slowly and for a long time—as if you were braising a veal shank.

Start by cutting the ends off of some carrots. You can choose to either peel the carrots or scrub them clean if they don't seem too dirty. Either way, you want to cut them into big pieces. Then, brown the carrots in olive oil and butter, which gives them a lot of flavor. You don't need to brown them too much; you just want them to develop a sweet caramelization, which is a result of the sugar found in those carrots that is beginning to brown.

After the carrots are browned, build a braise by adding some more oil and onions to the pan. Cook the onions until they're translucent and then add some celery and a smashed clove of garlic to the pan. In a long-simmered dish like osso buco, that one flattened clove of garlic will cook into a velvety puree over the span of an hour. Stir in a little bit of tomato paste and cook it just long enough to take the bright color out of it and give it some depth of flavor. Then, add a bouquet garni—holding a bay leaf, thyme, and parsley—and a few slices of orange with the zest intact, which will give an aromatic bitterness that will taste of oranges. Then, add some tomato concassé (peeled, seeded, and diced tomatoes). Depending on the time of the year, you may use canned or fresh tomatoes.

After adding the vegetables, if the pan seems dry, you can add some chicken or vegetable stock, depending on whether you want this to be a vegetarian dish. Season the dish with salt and pepper. Then, spread everything out evenly in the pan and cover the braise with a tight-fitting lid to keep the moisture in. The sauce should come about halfway up the side of the pan—just as if you were braising a piece of meat.

Turn the temperature down and let the braise simmer for about an hour. Every 10 to 15 minutes, stir the braise and turn the pieces of carrots over to make sure that they cook evenly. You don't want the pan to go dry, so if it's cooking faster than expected, add a splash of water.

After about an hour, take out both the bouquet garni and the slices of orange. The sauce should be thick but still liquid. The onions should be tender, and the tomatoes should begin to fall apart. Taste the sauce and, if it is still a little bit sweet, add a few drops of lemon juice.

This carrot osso buco could be a vegetarian entrée, but you could also serve it with a piece of chicken or steak. The great thing about this dish is that it can be cooked a few days in advance and then reheated very gently on top of the stove with a splash of extra water.

When you make a dish that is braised—whether it contains meat or vegetables— the dish gains a tremendous complexity and depth of flavor. However, you lose vitality and freshness because it is cooked for so long. To put vitality back into this dish, top it with gremolata, which involves chopped parsley, finely diced lemon zest, and crushed garlic. When you mix these three ingredients together, you end up with a mixture that has aromatic, fresh, vital flavor. It has the grassy sweetness of parsley; the sharp, aromatic citrusy quality of lemon zest; and the bite of garlic.

A Few Great Desserts
for Grown-Ups
Lesson 22

In this lesson, you will be introduced to a grown-up's approach to dessert—an approach that doesn't involve too much sweetness in the form of caramel, chocolate, and gooey icing. Instead, you will learn to have an appreciation for perfectly ripe fruit with just enough sweetness added to it to make it taste great (not to mention the addition of some high-proof alcohol). You will learn how to make several simple desserts with a single preparation that you can have on hand in your pantry.

Bachelor's Jam

Shopping List

proportions to taste

fresh berries
sugar

high-proof alcohol

The perfect time of the year to make this jam is during the summer when you can easily obtain ripe, fresh berries—including raspberries, blackberries, red currants, blueberries, peaches, and nectarines.

After you have selected some fresh fruit, combine all of it in a bowl, and for every pound of fruit, add about a cup of sugar. You may decide that more sugar is appropriate, especially if you use a lot of currants, which are very acidic and sharp. Then, cover the fruit with a high-proof alcohol (something that is 80 proof or more), such as rum, kirsch, eau-de-vie, vodka, brandy, cognac, or Armagnac.

Once you add the liquor, cover the bowl and set it aside for a minimum of two to three weeks. The fruit will flavor the spirits, but the spirits will also preserve the fruit. You don't have to worry about refrigerating the fruit-and-spirits mixture; you can just put it in a canning jar and leave it on the shelf in your pantry.

After about two or three weeks, taste the jam. Once it tastes good to you, you can eat it as it is with a spoon, but you can also do a few things to refine it. First, if you're concerned about your health, you can create a dessert that involves Greek yogurt with the fruit-and-spirits mixture on top. To add a little texture, add some toasted almonds as well.

If you are looking for a dessert that is a bit fancier, put a dollop of whipped cream that is sweetened with a little bit of vanilla in the bottom of a large dish. Then, place the jam around the cream so that you can see the beautiful colors of the jam. Then, add a few pieces of angel food cake to the dish.

Finally, you can make a parfait with the jam by ladling the jam into the bottom of a tall coffee mug. Then, add a layer of granola and top it off with a dollop of cream. Make sure that you have a long spoon that can reach the bottom of the mug.

As you use the jam, if more berries become available, then simply add them to the container that you are storing the jam in, add some sugar, and top it off with some spirits. You don't have to worry about the jam spoiling because the high-proof alcohol is a great preservative.

Bachelor's jam is wonderfully aromatic and fruity because of the alcohol that it contains, so you can pair it with a cheese that is equally aromatic: washed-rind cheese, such as limburger, muenster, and époisses de bourgogne. When these cheeses reach the point at which they need to be aged, their outsides are bathed in liquid, which creates the perfect environment for a particular bacteria that grows red, pink, or orange and is very aromatic.

Summer Pudding

Another way to use bachelor's jam is in summer pudding, which is made in England at the height of the summer season when berries are abundant.

To make summer pudding, start by making a fruit compote. Place a pan on the stove on high heat and sprinkle some sugar into it. Once the pan is hot, the sugar will begin to melt and then it will start to color. You have to constantly stir it. It would be ideal for all of the sugar to melt at once.

bachelor's jam
sugar
red wine
fresh berries
cinnamon sticks

a clove or a pinch
   of powdered cloves
salt
stale bread
whipped cream
mint leaves

Sugar melts at about 300 degrees, and shortly after that, it will begin to brown and caramelize, resulting in a much fuller, richer flavor than sugar has on its own. As the sugar begins to brown, you will first notice a golden color; then, the golden color will give way to a brown color. Continue to cook it until you see it just start to become reddish, which tells you that the flavor will be complexly sweet and bitter. If at any point the sugar seems to be browning too quickly, pull it off the heat and allow it to keep browning with just the heat that is inherent in the sugar.

As soon as you notice some smoke coming off the pan and the sugar seems to be done caramelizing, bring the temperature down with the introduction of a little bit of liquid in the form of red wine. When you add liquid to the hot sugar, be careful because you can expect a big puff of steam to result. In addition, the molten sugar will almost immediately firm up again, but it will continue to cook and dissolve little by little. Then, add some fresh berries—including blackberries, strawberries, blueberries, and raspberries—to the liquid and cook them until they begin to come apart, soften, and give up their juice.

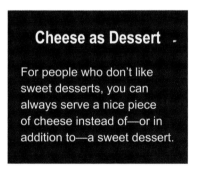

Cheese as Dessert

For people who don't like sweet desserts, you can always serve a nice piece of cheese instead of—or in addition to—a sweet dessert.

In addition to the flavor of the red wine and the caramel, add a few cinnamon sticks and a single clove (or a pinch of powdered cloves) to the pan. While the contents of the pan come up to a simmer, add a pint of bachelor's jam. Then, let the contents of the pan simmer for about 10 minutes, which is about how long it takes for the fruit to give up its flavor.

After about 10 minutes, taste the fruit compote. It should be slightly reduced and should have a full, rich flavor. Add a pinch of salt to round out the flavor.

Summer pudding involves mixing the berry compote with stale bread. To prepare the bread, cut the crusts off and then line a bowl with the bread. It is best to cut the bread into small wedges, or you can tear the bread into pieces that you think are just about the right size.

After the bowl is lined with bread, introduce some of the fruit compote and the juices that have come from the fruit as well. As the bread absorbs the juice, the bread will turn a deep color and swell, and all the little gaps will fill in with fruit and juice. Next, add a second layer of small bits and pieces of bread and top it with more fruit. Make sure that you are generous with the juices. Add another layer of bread, filling in the gaps, and another layer of fruit. Then, use some big slices of bread to piece together a lid that spans the bowl and is roughly semicircular.

Wine-and-Cheese Pairing

Pairing wine and cheese is not as easy as you might think it is. There are plenty of reasons that wine and cheese go well together, but there are plenty of reasons that they don't. For example, maybe a particular cheese coats your palate and the wine can't get through, or maybe a cheese has so much savory flavor that it just makes the wine seem awkward and strong.

Finally, cover the top layer of bread with enough liquid so that all of the bread can absorb the flavorful juices and begin to swell. Don't be stingy with the juice because you want the bread to be completely soaked with it. Make sure that you are using a large bowl in case the juices spill over, and you can even put the bowl on a plate so if the juices do spill over, they will be caught by the plate. Then, top the bread with a generous amount of fruit as well.

Once the bread has had a chance to absorb the juice, put a plate on top of the bread and press it down with a can of tomato juice or a can of tomatoes. Then, set it aside. Eventually, the bread will turn completely purple. At that point, you can place a plate upside down on top of the summer pudding and then flip the whole bowl over so that the summer pudding ends up on the plate. You may discover that as the bread swells, it forms a seal, so you may have to break the vacuum by putting a knife or spoon between the edge of the bowl and the pudding.

To make this dessert more attractive, decorate it with some fresh berries, so you might want to think about saving some before making the compote. When you are ready to serve the summer pudding, use a sharp knife to cut wedges out of the pudding. Present it whole with a little bit of whipped cream and a few leaves of mint on the side.

Pineapple-and-Banana Butter

Shopping List

proportions to taste

pineapple, cut	water
banana, peeled and cut	cinnamon sticks
brown sugar	lime zest

Pineapple-and-banana butter is similar to apple butter, except for the fact that it involves pineapple and banana instead of apple. Start with some pineapple and ripe banana that have been peeled, cut, put into a blender, and pureed. Then, add the pureed mixture to a large, flat pan. In a separate pan, mix some brown sugar with water and heat it until it dissolves. Then, add the dissolved brown sugar to the pan with the pureed mixture in it. Finally, add a few cinnamon sticks and a good deal of lime zest.

Put this mixture into the oven at a low temperature—between 250 and 300 degrees—and cook it for about three hours. After that amount of time, the volume will be reduced and the mixture will begin to caramelize, resulting in full flavor. Make sure to stir the mixture periodically, scraping the sides of the pan so that none of it burns. As it gets close to being done, watch it very carefully because it can burn easily.

Dessert Wines

Dessert wines are foolproof when paired with cheese. In making an ice wine, the fruit is actually frozen, which concentrates the sugars and gives a sweet, concentrated, dense flavor. Botrytized wines are wines in which a particular mold infects the grapes to give them a wonderful concentration of fruit flavors and new flavors, like honey, that weren't there before.

Once the butter cools, evaluate its consistency. If it feels a little bit thick or sticky, you can add a little water to thin it out. Then, you can put it in a jar. The butter will become a deep russet or mahogany color that is similar to the color of apple butter.

Pineapple-and-banana butter goes well with salty, aged cheeses. As an example, try it with an aged goat's milk gouda called Midnight Moon. The combination of the salty cheese—which has a caramel flavor to it, along with savory overtones—and the butter is spectacular. You won't even reach for bread; just add a little bit of the butter to the top of the cheese.

Honeycomb, Blue Cheese, and Hazelnut

Shopping List

proportions to taste

hazelnuts, toasted
blue cheese
honeycomb or honey

You can think of this combination as the best candy bar you will ever eat. Start with some toasted hazelnuts and a piece of blue cheese. Then, cut just a little bit of honeycomb to accompany those two items. You don't have to use honeycomb, but if you can find it, honeycomb is better to use than honey. Eat all three in tandem, and when you get the combination right, you will experience the salty, savory, creamy qualities of the cheese side by side with the aromatic honey that is sweet and complex and, finally, the roasted crunch of the nuts. For your second bite, you can choose to add more or less of any of the three ingredients to match your particular taste.

Thirst—The New Frontier of Flavor

Lesson 23

Many people often decide what they are going to eat and then, as an afterthought, choose a wine to accompany the food. Imagine for a second that wine is not just the beverage you use to wash down what you eat but, instead, that it is liquid flavor. If you think of wine as an ingredient, then you can understand that wine is an integral part of a more compelling dining experience. Thirst—not hunger—is the new frontier of flavor, and if you pay attention to wine, there's a lot that you can learn about flavor interaction that will improve your cooking.

Shopping List

proportions to taste

sauvignon blanc	salt
chardonnay	unseasoned steak, medium-rare
pinot noir	lemon
cabernet sauvignon	dill
sautéed salmon with tomato and basil	tarragon
	goat cheese
sugar	cream cheese

Tasting Exercise: Wine-and-Food Pairing

For this tasting exercise, you will need a sauvignon blanc, a chardonnay, a pinot noir, and a cabernet sauvignon. It will also be best if you have the following ingredients: sautéed salmon with tomato and basil, sugar, salt, an unseasoned steak that is cooked medium-rare, lemon, dill, tarragon, goat cheese, and cream cheese.

Sauvignon Blanc

First, you should taste the sauvignon blanc to understand what it tastes like. Start by sniffing it, and even before you taste it, you can appreciate the quality in the wine by the way it smells. Wine as an ingredient is a pretty compelling ingredient. It's aromatic, complex, and changeable over time—not to mention delicious.

Before you taste the wine, try to decide what you smell. You should find a quality about the wine that is green. It might smell vaguely like green apples and green herbs, such as sage. If you want to make the wine more aromatic, you can swirl it in the wine glass, but an appropriate glass is designed to funnel the aroma right up to your nose.

Then, taste the wine. Does it taste different than it smells? It should also taste pretty green, and there should be a lot of bright acidity in the wine. It might even taste like underripe fruit, such as a tart green apple. Ask yourself the following questions: Is the wine sweet? No, it should be acidic. Is the wine alcoholic? Not really. Is there a lot of tannin in the wine drying your mouth out? No, there shouldn't be. In addition to green apple, the wine might taste bitter—almost like grapefruit, lemon, or lime.

Once you have tasted the wine and have familiarized your palate with the flavor of the wine, then you can move on to pairing it with food. After tasting the wine, taste the food to see what qualities the food has, and then taste the wine again and see how your perception of the wine may have changed because of the food that you ate.

Taste just a little bit of goat cheese. Before you move on, ask yourself how the goat cheese tastes. It's acidic in its own right. There's a grassiness, or herbaceous, quality to it. It washes off your palate very quickly. It's not creamy. There's a mineral quality—sort of a chalkiness—to goat cheese.

Next, taste the wine and note how it changes. The acidity in the wine speaks to the tartness of the goat cheese. There is a mineral quality in the wine that plays off the mineral quality and chalkiness of the goat cheese. In addition, the herbaceous quality of the cheese, the grassiness, speaks to the green, herbaceous flavor in the wine.

Finally, take a little bit of dill and add it to the goat cheese so that you taste goat cheese with green, grassy herbs. You'll know when you get the combination right because it will taste good to you. Then, taste the wine again. You should notice a much more compelling match. There's something about the dill that speaks to the green flavors in the wine. The food itself tastes more complex, and when you pair it with the wine, the complexity increases.

You should also taste something that doesn't go very well with this wine so that you can compare it to the taste of goat cheese. Taste some cream cheese. While goat cheese and cream cheese look very similar to one another, they couldn't be more different. The goat cheese is tart; the cream cheese is sweet

and buttery. The goat cheese washes off your palate very quickly; the cream cheese coats your palate with a buttery richness and creaminess. There's none of the herbaceous quality in cream cheese that goat cheese has.

Then, taste the wine after having tasted the cream cheese. Right away, you get a tremendous pushback—the wine suddenly shocks you. The flavor has completely changed. The sweetness of the cream cheese made the wine seem more aggressive.

Chardonnay

Chardonnay is a very different wine from sauvignon blanc. It tends to be a lot softer and rounder, riper, and not nearly as acidic. When you smell it, you should smell sweet, round flavors. You might smell ripe apples—not green apples. You might even smell a little bit of pineapple, some creaminess that comes from malolactic fermentation, and a vanilla flavor that typically comes from oak.

Wine Acidity

When you're looking for acidity in a wine, you should look for a mouthwatering quality. Your body has a certain pH, and if you take something in—such as wine—that is at a different pH from your body, your body will respond by trying to balancing things again. With acidic wine, you should experience a flood of saliva, which waters down the acidity. An acidic, or tart, wine is a mouthwatering wine.

Then, taste the wine. It should not be nearly as acidic as the sauvignon blanc was. It should taste of riper fruit and have a rounder body and fuller flavor. Even though this is a dry wine, it tends to be a little bit sweet on the palate. It's a bigger wine with more alcohol, and there is a little bit of tannin in this wine because it has seen some oak.

This time, start by tasting the cream cheese. Then, taste the wine again. This experience should be reminiscent of tasting the goat cheese with the sauvignon blanc. The sweetness of the cream cheese speaks to the sweetness in the wine. You should taste the ripe fruit, the soft acidity, and the little bit of creaminess and butteriness.

Focus this combination by adding a leaf of tarragon to a small bite of cream cheese. Tarragon is sweet, and it has an anise flavor. It's very soft, and there is a little bit of vanilla in tarragon. After you chew this combination so that you can taste everything, taste the wine again. There is something really compelling about the creaminess and butteriness of the cheese side by side with the flavor of tarragon that really makes the wine shine.

Pinot Noir

Pinot noir is a very aromatic wine; it is known for its aroma. When you smell it, this wine might remind you of cherry cough drops or of a dusty rose. It smells a little bit floral. When you taste it, you will find that this wine is much bigger than the first two wines. There is some tannin, but there's also some very ripe, soft fruit. The acidity is higher than you might expect for a red wine; it has some bright acidity.

After you taste the pinot noir, taste some salmon, which is a mild fish that is very rich with oil. Add a little bit of salt to the salmon. On your palate, the weight and intensity of flavor is almost identical to those qualities found in the wine. The richness of the fish is cut by the acidity in the wine, and there's something about the aroma of pinot noir that speaks to the fish.

Next, focus the combination by adding tomato and basil to the salted salmon. After you taste the combination, taste the wine again. The sweet spice from the basil brings out some sweetness in the wine. The tomato is a fruit, so it echoes the taste of ripe fruit in the wine.

Acidity is important in wine, and it's also important with food. The pinot noir has a pretty high acidity level, and the fish with tomatoes has a lower acidity level, so you can add lemon juice to the fish to bring the acidity level up to equal what you find in the wine. After you add a few drops of lemon juice to the salted fish

with tomato and basil and take a bite, you might notice that the fish tastes better. After tasting the wine again, you will find that this is a pretty compelling match. Be careful that the level of acidity in your food does not go beyond the level of acidity that you find in your wine.

Cabernet Sauvignon

Cabernet sauvignon is very opaque and dark. It is heavily extracted. By looking at it, you would expect it to be a big wine. It smells only partially of fruit; it actually smells like the plant that the fruit grows on, such as the leaves of blackberries. When you taste it, you might taste a hint of tobacco, dark fruit, and a vegetal quality. It is not very acidic; it's a very full-flavored wine. There's quite a bit of tannin, but it's also smooth and delicious.

After tasting the wine, eat a little piece of unseasoned steak that is cooked medium-rare. Then, taste the wine. The wine should seem stronger, less fruity, more astringent, more tannic, and less sweet. The problem is that the steak is not seasoned. As it is, it's an expression of pure savory flavor, or umami, which can make wine taste strong—but not in a good way. Add some salt to the steak, and then taste it again. It should taste better after being seasoned. Then, taste the wine again. Everything that was right about the wine earlier should come racing back. It is now fruity, soft, round, balanced, and very appealing.

Seasoning is an important consideration. For example, when you add sweet food to dry wines, the combination is not very appealing. Sugar can make wine taste stronger and aggressive, less fruity, more acidity, more tannic, and more astringent. Try adding sugar to your palate and then tasting a dry wine, such as cabernet sauvignon.

The Seven Deadly Sins of Wine-and-Food Pairing

The seven deadly sins of wine-and-food pairing are seven types of food that are hard on wine and, for that reason, should be avoided. However, once you know what the issue is with the food, you can often find a solution. The seven deadly sins are chiles, vinegar, eggs, spinach, artichokes, asparagus, and soup.

Chiles are an irritant. Tannin, alcohol, acidity, and astringency are all irritants. If you rough up your palate with too much spicy food, wine can hurt, but when you find spicy food on your plate, choose a wine that has low alcohol, no astringency, no tannin, and maybe a little bit of sweetness.

Vinegar is spoiled wine, and it makes sense that you shouldn't pair spoiled wine with wine. However, if you add vinegar to a stew to make it less rich and more acidic, because vinegar does not define the dish, it shouldn't be a problem to drink wine with that dish. In that case, vinegar is simply a seasoning, but if you add so much vinegar to a dish that it dominates the dish, then that dish will probably not go well with wine.

Eggs have a coating quality that can coat your palate, especially when they are a bit undercooked, and with a coated palate, wine will just slip right by and you won't even notice it. What you may notice is that there is a sulfurous compound in eggs that can play up the sulfur that is inherent in the wine-making process, and it becomes unpleasant. Instead, consider putting eggs into a quiche, which is defined by the roasted and buttery flavor of the crust and by the cheese, bacon, and onions. Because eggs don't define a quiche, it should be fine to drink wine with it.

The Six Steps of Wine-and-Food Pairing

1. Taste the wine and make sure you know what defines that particular type of wine.
2. Pay attention to the weight and intensity of the wine.
3. Decide what you're going to cook—what's going to define your food.
4. Choose a cooking technique; each distinct technique will bring something different to your food.
5. Build relationships between the food and wine to bring the match into focus.
6. Season the food appropriately so that when the food is properly seasoned, the wine tastes great.

Spinach has a compound called oxalic acid that can make wine seem sort of metallic, so when you eat spinach, make sure that you redefine it in some meaningful way. For example, a few leaves of spinach added to a stir-fry or spinach that is sautéed with garlic and herbs would not be a problem in terms of pairing spinach with wine.

Artichokes can make wine taste sweet because of an enzyme called cymarin. Therefore, you should steam artichokes, take off the petals, and dip them into mayonnaise. It's less important what you dip into the mayonnaise and more important what the mayonnaise tastes like. If you remove the heart of an artichoke, cut it up, and add it as a garnish in a veal or lamb stew, for example, you can still drink wine with that dish—which is all about the deep, rich flavor of the stew and not about the few pieces of artichoke that you added to it.

Asparagus can make wine taste awkward by almost robbing it of its fruity qualities. To redefine the asparagus, you could cook it so that it becomes defined by the cooking technique that you choose to use. If you grill it, you will taste the char and a little bit of smokiness, and if you sprinkle some parmesan cheese and some thyme on top, you might not even recognize it as asparagus anymore and can certainly drink wine with it.

Soup is basically a beverage, and in classical French cuisine, you would not pair a wine with soup because it would be a beverage paired with a beverage. However, this guideline probably refers to clear soup, such as a consommé. If you have a rich, hearty soup—such as a minestrone with cheese and olive oil on top—and you eat it with another piece of cheese or with some crusty bread, there are plenty of wines that you could find that could be paired with it.

Crafting a Meal, Engaging the Senses
Lesson 24

This course has focused on three broad themes: taste and flavor, cooking techniques, and the importance of good-quality ingredients. In this lesson, you will learn that it is not simple to leverage those three ideas into a meal. Cooking is a craft that has to be practiced in order to elevate it to become an art form. While you are practicing, keep in mind that every chef wishes that he or she were a better chef, and there's always an opportunity tomorrow to become that better chef.

Spanish Tortilla with Aioli

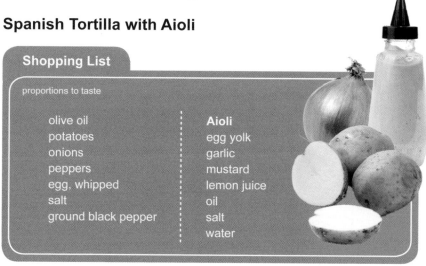

Shopping List

proportions to taste

olive oil	**Aioli**
potatoes	egg yolk
onions	garlic
peppers	mustard
egg, whipped	lemon juice
salt	oil
ground black pepper	salt
	water

A Spanish tortilla, unlike a Mexican tortilla, is akin to an omelet. To make a Spanish tortilla, start by cooking some potatoes, onions, and peppers in a lot of olive oil. Cook the potatoes until they are on their way to being tender and then add some onions and peppers. Continue to cook all three ingredients until they are completely tender. Don't cook the potatoes in heat that is too high because you don't want them to brown; instead, cook them gently so that they can absorb the wonderful flavor of the olive oil. It is better to overcook the potatoes than to undercook them.

Once the potatoes, onions, and peppers have cooked and then cooled down, bind them with just enough egg so that they will hold together. If you use too much egg, this dish will become a little bit rubbery. Before you add the vegetables to the egg, whip the egg. Then, season the mixture with salt and pepper.

Introduce some olive oil to a hot nonstick pan. Then, add the egg mixture to the pan. Make sure that the pan is hot so that the mixture sets on the outside. If the pan is hot, the omelet will slide easily in the pan and not get stuck anywhere. However, you should turn down the heat of the pan because you don't want the omelet to cook too aggressively; you don't want it burnt on the bottom by the time it starts to cook in the middle. Adjust the heat so that you see some bubbling around the edges.

After about five minutes, you will notice that the eggs begin to set and the omelet slides freely in the pan. At that point, you can take a plate that's slightly bigger than the omelet and slide the omelet out of the pan and onto the plate. Then, flip the omelet over and put the pan back on the heat. Introduce a little more oil to the pan and slide the omelet back into the pan. While the omelet is still a little soft, shape the edges by folding them underneath the omelet so that it comes out round. Cook the omelet on its second side over a very gentle heat for about 5 to 10 minutes—until the center is firm. In other words, the eggs should be cooked all the way through.

The sauce that accompanies this Spanish tortilla is a garlic mayonnaise called aioli. To a bowl, add one egg yolk, which will provide the emulsifiers that will allow lemon juice and oil to combine when they ordinarily don't. The egg yolk should be warm, as should all of the ingredients. Next, add a little bit of garlic and some mustard to the bowl. Then, add just a few drops of lemon juice.

To establish an emulsion, drizzle in some oil, drop by drop, while you whip the ingredients aggressively. As you add more oil, the mixture should become thicker and thicker. As soon as the mixture starts to look creamy and a little thick, an emulsion has begun to form. The process of making hollandaise sauce is very similar to this process—except rather than using oil, you use butter to make hollandaise sauce.

Once the emulsion is established, you don't have to worry about how quickly you are adding the oil, but if the mixture ever starts looking greasy, that means that you are adding too much oil too quickly. Early in the process, stop whipping for a second to season the mixture with salt. Because it becomes very thick, sometimes it is difficult for the salt to dissolve if you add it too late in the process.

At some point, you might decide that you want to thin this mixture out, which you can do by adding a small amount of liquid. Even with only a few drops of lemon juice, you will noticeably see how the mayonnaise begins to relax. If you reach a point where you can't add any more lemon juice because it is already too tart, you can relax it with a little bit of water instead.

For one yolk, you will end up using about a half a cup of oil. If you use too little oil, your mayonnaise will taste of egg yolk and cling to your pallet in an unpleasant way. If you use too much oil, the mayonnaise will taste only of oil and not much else. When you think you have whipped the mayonnaise enough, taste it and add extra lemon juice, water, and garlic as needed.

When the Spanish tortilla is done cooking, slide it out of the pan and cut it into about eight pieces before you serve it on a plate. Don't add the mayonnaise until right before you are ready to serve. Because this dish tastes great at room temperature, you can make it well ahead of time. Keep the mayonnaise in the refrigerator, but the tortilla can be kept at room temperature for about three or four hours.

Gnocchi with Pesto Sauce

To make gnocchi with pesto sauce, begin by making the pesto. Into a food processor, add lots of basil, which is very aromatic. Then, add a few cloves of garlic and some

Gnocchi Variations

Instead of covering your gnocchi in pesto sauce, you can also make gnocchi with brown butter, sage, and a little bit of parmesan cheese. Gnocchi also tastes delicious with cream, gorgonzola cheese, and maybe even some toasted walnuts.

toasted pine nuts and start the process of grinding the mixture down. While the food processor runs, introduce some good-quality olive oil. Scrape the sides of the food processor with a spatula so that it grinds evenly. Season the mixture with a lot of salt and some pepper. Add some cheese at the very end because sometimes the ingredients can heat up in a food processor, and if it gets too hot, the cheese can melt and become problematic.

You can make the pesto well in advance. It keeps really well, so if you make a batch, make a large batch and put some in the freezer. If you freeze it, top it with some extra olive oil so that it won't oxidize. You can refrigerate it if you think you will use it up within about a week.

To make the gnocchi, boil some russet potatoes in a large pot of water. Once they are boiled and drained from the water, put them on a sheet pan and pop them into a 350-degree oven for 5 to 10 minutes so that they can steam dry. Then, rice the potatoes and season the resulting dough with salt and pepper. Also add a pinch of nutmeg and some parmesan cheese. Make a small well inside the dough and add a few eggs to the center, mixing them into the dough. Then, introduce enough flour so that the dough becomes moist—but not sticky.

The secret to making a light gnocchi is to make sure not to overknead the dough, but a certain amount of kneading is essential so that the dough will stick together and hold its shape when you start to roll out the gnocchi.

Take a portion of the dough and roll it out—on a floured surface—into a log. When you are rolling the dough into a log, it is more about finesse than power. Feel for the areas that are a little bit thicker and put a little bit of pressure on those areas. If the log becomes too long, cut it in half and carry on. Cut the log into three-quarter-inch pieces. When you cook the gnocchi, they will grow to about twice their original size, so don't cut them too large. Then, briefly roll each of the pieces around to break the hard edges on the outside. Try to find someone you can share the labor with during this part of the cooking.

After you cut the gnocchi into pieces, put them onto a floured sheet pan so that they don't stick. Then, shape them by using a gnocchi board that is ridged on one side or by using a fork. Roll the gnocchi down the ridge of the board or the fork with your thumb, lightly pushing your thumb down and forward.

If you were to add the gnocchi to a pot of water without making those ridges, it would take a long time to cook because of the thickness of the gnocchi. The outside would become soft, the inside would take its time to cook, and it would be a little bit slimy and unpleasant. When you make ridges on the gnocchi, you are adding texture on the outside, but you are also creating a little dimple on the back of the gnocchi where your thumb pressed on it. Basically, you have flattened it out so that it cooks quicker, and you have made a little hollow that will accept sauce.

Drop the gnocchi into a pot of boiling water. At first, they should sink to the bottom, which is indicative of their being fairly dense, but as they cook, they will become lighter and less dense and should float to the top of the water. They should also hold their shape. As soon as they float to the top, remove them from the water.

To make the pesto sauce that accompanies the gnocchi, add a dollop of the premade pesto to some pasta water in a pan on high heat. This watery sauce will turn into a creamy, thick sauce as soon as the cooked gnocchi is added. While the sauce comes up to a simmer, the gnocchi will absorb all of the excess

moisture. As soon as the sauce develops an appropriate consistency, add a little bit of cheese to the pan and slide the gnocchi onto a dish, sprinkling some more cheese and some fresh black pepper on top.

You can make gnocchi ahead of time—and you should. You can also freeze them in an open pan so that they don't stick together, and then, after they are frozen, you can put them into a ziplock bag. When you are ready to serve the gnocchi, accompany it with a simple tomato salad topped with basil, which is a great match for the potato in the gnocchi and the pesto.

Turnovers with Pineapple-and-Banana Butter

Shopping List

proportions to taste

puff pastry or pie dough
flour
pineapple-and-banana
  butter (Lesson 22)

egg wash
ice cream

Food-and-Wine Pairing

To accompany this meal, pinot noir is the best wine to choose. It complements potatoes, tomatoes, and the sweet spice that is found in pesto. For dessert, pour some botrytized dessert wine, which is a great match for the turnovers or a simple cookie, such as shortbread with lavender and orange. Because the turnovers have fruit in them, they are great when combined with a dry cheese, such as gouda or dry monterey jack.

To make these turnovers, start by rolling some commercial puff pastry on the thinner side because you want to make the turnovers fairly small. When you roll from the center to the outside, you need to make sure that the pastry is moving as you roll, and if it doesn't, then make sure that there is plenty of flour underneath it so that it can slide rather than stick.

Once the dough has been rolled out, cut it into three-inch squares and put a small dollop of pineapple-and-banana butter on each. Then, so that the sides of the turnovers stick together, brush them with some egg wash, which is egg that has been beaten with about a tablespoon of water.

To shape the turnovers, bring the pastry up and over the filling, trying to make sure that it seals completely so that there are no air pockets. If you want to put a decorative edge on it, you can do that by simply pressing down lightly on the edge with a fork. If you can't make a puff pastry or pie dough to make these turnovers—or you want to save some time—check to see if a local bakery can make it for you.

Next, transfer the turnovers to a pan so that they can bake. Give each one some room in the pan so that the heat can circulate all around it. Before they go into the oven, brush them with some egg wash so that they have a nice shine and brown nicely. Don't use too much egg wash because you don't want them to be sitting in a pool of scrambled eggs once they bake. Try to avoid coating the cut edge of the dough because it will rise much more effectively if the cut edge is not glued together with egg.

Because they are small, bake the turnovers at about 400 degrees. They will bake fairly quickly. The dough should get a chance to brown nicely—not just on the top, but on the bottom as well. The egg will brown easily, but you also want the pastry to brown and become crisp. Because the dough has layers upon layers of pastry, as it bakes, it will puff up. After about 15 minutes, the turnovers should be done baking. When you are ready to eat them, serve them with ice cream.

Recipe List

Bibliography

Note: All books listed below are available on the website of The Culinary Institute of America at http://www.ciaprochef.com/fbi/enthusiasts.html.

Conniff-Dobrich, Cate. *Seasons in the Wine Country: Recipes from The Culinary Institute of America at Greystone*. San Francisco: Chronicle Books, 2010.

Coppedge, Richard J., Jr. *Gluten-Free Baking with The Culinary Institute of America: 150 Flavorful Recipes from the World's Premier Culinary College*. Holbrook, MA: Adams Media, 2008.

The Culinary Institute of America. *Baking at Home with The Culinary Institute of America*. New York: Wiley, 2004.

———. *Breakfasts & Brunches*. New York: Lebhar-Friedman, 2005.

———. *Cookies at Home with The Culinary Institute of America*. New York: Wiley, 2011.

———. *Cooking at Home with The Culinary Institute of America*. New York: Wiley, 2003.

———. *The Culinary Institute of America Cookbook: A Collection of Our Favorite Recipes for the Home Chef*. New York: Lebhar-Friedman, 2008.

———. *Gourmet Meals in Minutes*. New York: Lebhar-Friedman, 2004.

———. *Grilling: Exciting International Flavors from the World's Premier Culinary College*. New York: Lebhar-Friedman, 2006.

———. *Healthy Cooking at Home with The Culinary Institute of America*. New York: Wiley, 2011.

———. *The New Book of Soups*. New York: Lebhar-Friedman, 2009.

———. *One Dish Meals*. New York: Lebhar-Friedman, 2006.

———. *The Professional Chef*. 9th ed. New York: Wiley, 2011. (The online version of this book can be found at https://www.inkling.com/store/professional-chef-cia-9th/.)

————. *Vegetables.* New York: Lebhar-Friedman, 2007.

————, Mark Erickson, and Lisa Erickson. *Cooking for One: A Seasonal Guide to the Pleasure of Preparing Delicious Meals for Yourself.* New York: Lebhar-Friedman, 2011.

———— and Ben Fink. *Hors d'Oeuvre at Home with The Culinary Institute of America.* New York: Wiley, 2007.

———— and Darra Goldstein. *Baking Boot Camp: Five Days of Basic Training at The Culinary Institute of America.* New York: Wiley, 2007.

———— and Peter P. Greweling. *Chocolates & Confections at Home with The Culinary Institute of America.* New York: Wiley, 2009.

———— and Katherine Polenz. *Vegetarian Cooking at Home with The Culinary Institute of America.* New York: Wiley, 2012.

————, Gianni Scappin, Alberto Vanoli, and Steven Kolpan. *Italian Cooking at Home with The Culinary Institute of America.* New York: Wiley, 2011.

———— and Martha Rose Shulman. *Culinary Boot Camp: Five Days of Basic Training at The Culinary Institute of America.* New York: Wiley, 2006.

Fischer, John W., and Lou Jones. *Bistros and Brasseries: Recipes and Reflections on Classic Café Cooking.* New York: Lebhar-Friedman, 2008.

Kastel, Eric W., *Artisan Breads at Home.* New York: Wiley, 2010.

Scappin, Gianni, and Vincenzo Lauria. *A Tavola! Recipes and Reflections on Traditional Italian Home Cooking.* New York: Lebhar-Friedman, 2009.

Shulman, Martha Rose. *Spain and the World Table.* New York: DK Adult, 2011.

Photographic Credits

Page 146: © iStockphoto/Thinkstock, © Hemera/Thinkstock.
Page 147: © Stockbyte/Thinkstock, © Hemera/Thinkstock.
Page 148: © iStockphoto/Thinkstock.
Page 149: © iStockphoto/Thinkstock, © Hemera/Thinkstock, © Zoonar/Thinkstock.
Page 150: © iStockphoto/Thinkstock.
Page 152: © iStockphoto/Thinkstock, © Hemera/Thinkstock.
Page 153: © iStockphoto/Thinkstock.
Page 154: © iStockphoto/Thinkstock.
Page 156: © iStockphoto/Thinkstock, © Hemera/Thinkstock.
Page 158: © iStockphoto/Thinkstock.
Page 159: © Monkey Business/Thinkstock.
Page 160: © iStockphoto/Thinkstock.
Page 161: © iStockphoto/Thinkstock.
Page 162: © iStockphoto/Thinkstock.
Page 163: © iStockphoto/Thinkstock.
Page 164: © iStockphoto/Thinkstock.
Page 165: © iStockphoto/Thinkstock.
Page 166: © iStockphoto/Thinkstock, © Hemera/Thinkstock.
Page 167: © iStockphoto/Thinkstock.
Page 168: © iStockphoto/Thinkstock.
Page 170: © iStockphoto/Thinkstock, © Hemera/Thinkstock.
Page 172: © Monkey Business/Thinkstock.
Page 173: © iStockphoto/Thinkstock.
Page 174: © Zoonar/Thinkstock.
Page 175: © iStockphoto/Thinkstock, © Hemera Technologies/PhotoObjects.net/Thinkstock.
Page 176: © iStockphoto/Thinkstock, © Hemera/Thinkstock.
Page 177: © iStockphoto/Thinkstock.
Page 178: © Hemera/Thinkstock.
Page 179: © iStockphoto/Thinkstock.
Page 180: © iStockphoto/Thinkstock.
Page 181: © iStockphoto/Thinkstock.
Page 182: © iStockphoto/Thinkstock.
Page 185: © iStockphoto/Thinkstock.
Page 186: © iStockphoto/Thinkstock, © Marcy McDonald.
Page 187: © iStockphoto/Thinkstock.
Page 188: © iStockphoto/Thinkstock, © Hemera/Thinkstock.
Page 189: © iStockphoto/Thinkstock.
Page 190: © iStockphoto/Thinkstock, © Hemera Technologies/PhotoObjects.net/Thinkstock.
Page 191: © Marcy McDonald.
Page 192: © Martin Poole/Digital Vision/Thinkstock.
Page 196: © iStockphoto/Thinkstock.

200